SEVEN
TRADING
FLOORS OF
Heaven

CONFRONTING AND OVERCOMING
UNGODLY EXCHANGES

DR. ALDRIC MARSHALL

Published by: Dr. Aldric Marshall
Cover by: M A Rehman
Interior edited by: bookconversion

Printed in the United States of America
ISBN: 9798865067221

PRECAUTIONARY NOTE

The views, thoughts, and opinions expressed in this text belong solely to the author, and not necessarily to the author's employer, organization, committee, or other group or individual.

Readers are advised to exercise discretion while reading, particularly if the content could be triggering or sensitive to personal experiences.

Reproduction, copying, or any unauthorized use of the content without permission from the copyright holder is strictly prohibited. The publisher and the author assume no responsibility for any consequences arising from the use of the information herein.

Dedication

To the boundless love of my Heavenly Father, an eternal source of grace that envelops me each day; in memory of my beloved late mother, Elois Donaway, whose legacy shines as an enduring symbol of strength; to my treasured children, Kaleb and Keturah, whose unwavering spirits serve as my constant inspiration; to my steadfast brother and sister, whose unyielding loyalty knows no bounds; and to the dedicated community of believers at Connecting the World with the Word Ministries (CTW) — every one of you occupies a unique and cherished space within my heart and life's journey.

Your unwavering faith, tireless support, and unwavering presence have served as the North Star guiding me through life's most challenging waters and fiercest storms. This book stands as a testament to the profound imprint you've left on my soul and the unbreakable bonds we've woven together. As one united family and a formidable force, let us persist in facing and conquering the trials that life presents to us.

Table of Contents

INTRODUCTION

Seven Trading Floors of Heaven: Confronting and Overcoming Ungodly Exchanges

I n every whispered prayer, every choice made in solitude, every hushed promise, and in every heart's cry, there is a trade being made. As beings of volition and conscience, our lives are a continual series of exchanges, a ceaseless barter of values, intentions, and desires. Yet, while we remain acutely aware of our physical and material trades, there exists an underlying spiritual economy that often eludes our conscious grasp. "Trading Floors of Heaven: Confronting and Overcoming Ungodly Exchanges" delves into this very realm, unveiling the profound spiritual transactions that define our existence and destiny.

The concept of trading is not alien to our human experience. From the earliest days of barter systems to our current intricate global economy, trading is the lifeblood of human interaction. But as we navigate our earthly existence, are we aware of the unseen spiritual transactions we're making? Just as there are principles governing our physical trades, there are divine statutes overseeing our spiritual exchanges. This book is a journey into understanding these trades and ensuring they align with the heart and will of our Creator.

Our spiritual heritage, steeped in the wisdom of ancient scriptures, holds within it tales of trades that changed destinies. From Adam and Eve's fateful exchange in Eden to Esau's impulsive trade of his birthright, the Bible is replete with accounts that serve as both warnings and lessons. And yet, beyond these stories, lies a profound truth – our daily choices, knowingly or unknowingly, engage us in trades that have eternal repercussions.

But fear not, for this is not a message of despair. On the contrary, it's an invitation to enlightenment, to empowerment, and to spiritual rejuvenation. As you turn each page, you'll be equipped with the discernment to recognize negative trades and the wisdom to engage in exchanges that lead to blessings, purpose, and a closer walk with God.

"Seven Trading Floors of Heaven" is more than just a book; it's a spiritual compass, guiding you to confront and overcome the ungodly exchanges that have held you back. As we delve deep into the biblical understanding of trading, from the materialistic allure of Tyre to the seductive manipulations of Delilah, you'll be challenged to introspect, to recalibrate, and most importantly, to trade in line with God's divine economy.

In a world where voices clamor for our allegiance, where the lust for power, wealth, and recognition often clouds our judgment, this book is a clarion call to anchor ourselves in the eternal. It's a call to recognize that in every choice, in every sacrifice, and in every aspiration, there is an exchange happening on a spiritual level. The question is, are these trades drawing us closer to our Creator or leading us astray?

As you embark on this journey through the "Seven Trading Floors of Heaven," may you be inspired, transformed, and reoriented towards the heart of God. May you discover the true essence of value in God's divine economy and be filled with a renewed sense of purpose, passion, and spiritual vigor. Welcome to a voyage of eternal significance. Welcome to the trading floors of heaven.

CHAPTER 1

A Condemnation-Free Beginning

From the outset of the Judeo-Christian scriptures, we find a recurring theme: humanity's proclivity for trade-offs, exchanges, and negotiations, both with God and with each other. The concept of trading floors, in this context, represents the arenas or places where we make these spiritual and moral exchanges, often to our detriment. Yet, as we embark on this exploration, it's paramount to begin with the comforting assurance from the Apostle Paul in Romans 8:1, "There is therefore now no condemnation to them which are in Christ Jesus."

When we talk of 'trading floors', it's not about marketplaces or bazaars, but a metaphorical space representing our spiritual and moral decisions. To comprehend this fully, one must dive into the origins of trade as mentioned in the Bible. The word "trade" in Hebrew, "rakal," means to go about, a description quite pertinent to the wandering nature of our desires and the transactions we undertake to satisfy them.

Similarly, in the Greek Septuagint, one of the words translated as "trade" is "emporos," which refers to a merchant, emphasizing the idea of acquiring or exchanging.

The scriptures are replete with tales of such exchanges. Consider Esau, who exchanged his birthright for a mere bowl of stew, or Judas Iscariot, who traded his loyalty to Jesus for thirty pieces of silver. These biblical narratives underscore the profound implications of our trades, both for the individual and the broader community.

But why do we trade? At its core, trade arises from a perceived lack or a desire. Adam and Eve, in the garden of Eden, made the infamous trade when they were beguiled into thinking that God was withholding something from them. They traded their obedience and trust in God's word for the tantalizing allure of the serpent's promise, as narrated in Genesis 3. The consequence? An ejection from paradise and an introduction to a world where right and wrong trades could shape destinies.

Yet, in this discourse, it's crucial to shun any feelings of guilt or shame. Understanding our intrinsic nature to trade does not mean we stand condemned. On the contrary, recognizing these tendencies is the first step towards redemption. The scripture offers solace in Hebrews 4:15-16: *"For we do not have a high priest who is unable to empathize with our weaknesses, but we have one who has been tempted in every way, just as we are—yet he did not sin. Let us then approach God's throne of grace with confidence, so that we may receive mercy and find grace to help us in our time of need."*

Furthermore, Jesus, in the Gospels, frequently encountered individuals who had made poor trades in their lives. Whether it was Zacchaeus, the tax collector who had traded his integrity for wealth, or the woman at the well who had traded true love for fleeting relationships, Jesus never condemned them. Instead, He offered them a new trade: their brokenness for His redemption. As noted in Matthew 11:28-30, Jesus extends an invitation: "Come to me, all you who are weary and burdened, and I will give you rest. Take my yoke upon you and learn from me... For my yoke is easy and my burden is light."

Therefore, as we venture deeper into understanding the intricacies of these trading floors, it's essential to arm ourselves with the knowledge of God's boundless grace and mercy. We must remember that God's intent is not to condemn us but to bring us into a deeper revelation of His love and purposes.

This chapter has merely scratched the surface of the concept of trading floors. As we continue our exploration, we'll delve deeper into each specific trading floor, unearthing their implications, origins, and how they manifest in our lives. Through this journey, we'll not only discern the trades we've made but, more importantly, learn how to make trades that align with God's heart and design for our lives.

In this endeavor, we find encouragement in the words of Isaiah 55:2: "Why spend money on what is not bread, and your labor on what does not satisfy? Listen, listen to me, and eat what is good, and you will delight in the richest of fare." The scripture beckons us to evaluate our trades, reminding us that with God, the best exchange is yet to come.

TRADING FLOORS IN BIBLICAL LIVES

As we continue our journey into understanding the metaphorical trading floors, it becomes crucial to observe and reflect upon the real-life accounts from the scriptures. These narratives not only solidify the conceptual framework but also provide tangible examples, demonstrating how individuals have navigated their spiritual and moral exchanges with God and others.

1. **Solomon's Request:** One of the most profound trades in the Bible is found in the life of Solomon. As a young king succeeding his father David, Solomon was granted a unique opportunity. In a dream, God said to him, *"Ask for whatever you want me to give you"* (1 Kings 3:5). The magnitude of this proposition was colossal. Solomon could have asked for wealth, long life, or the lives of his enemies. Instead, he chose wisdom to govern God's people rightly. His request pleased the Lord, and as a result, Solomon was not only granted unparalleled wisdom but also wealth and honor. This tale accentuates the principle that when we prioritize God's will and the well-being of others in our trades, He blesses us abundantly beyond our initial request.

2. **Abraham and Lot:** Another poignant example comes from the life of Abraham and his nephew Lot. When their herders began to quarrel due to limited resources, Abraham proposed a trade. He gave Lot the choice of the land he wanted, whether to the left or to the right, even though, as the elder, Abraham had the prerogative to choose first. Lot, swayed by the lushness of the Jordan plain, chose it, leaving Abraham the seemingly less fertile land. But God's promise to Abraham remained, and he was blessed with the entire land, including the territories Lot had initially chosen (Genesis 13). Abraham's willingness to prioritize peace and relationship over material gain resulted in divine affirmation and blessing.

3. **The Rich Young Ruler:** Contrary to Solomon's wise trade, we find a sorrowful account of the rich young ruler in the New Testament. He approached Jesus with a sincere query

about inheriting eternal life. While he had adhered to the commandments, Jesus discerned the stronghold of wealth in his life. He was asked to sell everything, give to the poor, and follow Jesus (Mark 10:17-22). This trade seemed too steep for the ruler, and he walked away in grief. This story underscores that the trades we refuse can sometimes hold more consequence than those we undertake.

4. **Mary of Bethany:** In a tender moment recorded in the gospels, Mary of Bethany brought an alabaster jar of expensive perfume to anoint Jesus. This act was met with indignation by some present, citing the wastefulness of the act, as the perfume could have been sold for a significant sum and given to the poor (John 12:1-8). However, Jesus defended Mary's trade, recognizing it as an act of profound worship and love. She traded a valuable earthly possession for a heavenly affirmation. Mary's account serves as a beautiful reminder that trades made out of genuine love and reverence for God hold eternal significance.

5. **The Prodigal Son:** The parable of the prodigal son (Luke 15:11-32) is a stirring portrayal of misguided trades. The younger son traded his inheritance and his father's presence for fleeting pleasures in a distant land. However, when famine struck and he found himself destitute, he realized the folly of his trade. In a transformative moment of recognition, he decided to return to his father, expecting to be treated as a servant. Instead, he was met with a loving embrace and a grand celebration. The father traded his right to retribution for a relationship with his son. This parable encapsulates the heart of God towards us, ever-willing to redeem our poor trades when we turn back to Him.

6. **Moses:** Last but not least, the life of Moses presents a series of trades. Born a Hebrew but raised as an Egyptian prince, Moses had the luxuries of the palace. Yet, he chose to trade his royal standing to identify with his oppressed brethren, an act that led to his exile (Hebrews 11:24-27). Later, in his encounter with God at the burning bush, Moses traded his insecurities and self-doubt for a divine commission to lead Israel to freedom. His life exemplifies that trading temporal comforts for God's calling can lead to transformative destinies for oneself and many others.

Each of these biblical figures, through their trades, both wise and misguided, presents a mirror to our own lives. Their stories allow us to reflect on the exchanges we make daily, whether they align with God's design or stem from our desires and fears.

The biblical narrative, abundant with tales of trades, offers not only cautionary tales but also tales of hope. It reminds us that while we often err in our trades, there's a merciful God always ready to help us correct our course. As the Apostle Paul beautifully encapsulates in 2 Corinthians 5:21, *"God made him who had no sin to be sin for us, so that in him we might become the righteousness of God."* Here lies the greatest trade of all time: Jesus trading His righteousness for our sin, ensuring that even in our most regrettable trades, redemption remains within reach.

CHAPTER 2

The Inception of Trade

The genesis of humanity is deeply rooted in the pristine Garden of Eden, a setting where man existed in perfect communion with his Creator. Yet, even in this idyllic environment, the foundational trade that changed the trajectory of humanity took place. Through a seemingly simple act of eating forbidden fruit, Adam and Eve unknowingly embarked on a trade that would forever alter the essence of human nature.

To truly grasp the weight of their decision, we must understand the original context. In the garden, Adam and Eve were given dominion over all living creatures (Genesis 1:28). They existed in perfect unity with God, walking and talking with Him. But, crucially, they were also endowed with free will—a gift that, while allowing genuine love and obedience, also bore the potential for disobedience.

The Hebrew term "nachash" is often translated as "serpent" in Genesis 3. In ancient Near Eastern cultures, serpents symbolized cunning and deceit. When this nachash approached Eve, he posed a question that would instigate a profound trade: "Did God really say, 'You must not eat from any tree in the garden'?" (Genesis 3:1). This question was the first step in reshaping Eve's perspective. By introducing doubt about God's word and intent, the serpent set the stage for a trade of truth for deception.

Eve's response, while seemingly accurate, already began to diverge from God's original command. God had said, "You are free to eat from any tree in the garden; but you must not eat from the tree of the knowledge of good and evil, for when you eat from it you will certainly die" (Genesis 2:16-17). Yet, Eve added, *"and you must not touch it"* (Genesis 3:3). This addition, while minor, indicates a shift, a departure from the exactness of God's words.

The serpent, sensing this vulnerability, offered a tantalizing trade. *"You will not certainly die,"* he countered, *"For God knows that when you eat from it your eyes will be opened, and you will be like God, knowing good and evil"* (Genesis 3:4-5). Here, the nachash effectively proposed a trade of God-given contentment and security for the allure of god-like knowledge and autonomy.

Swayed by the serpent's words and the appealing nature of the fruit, Eve made the trade. She took and ate, and then offered it to Adam, who without recorded hesitation, did the same. The Greek Septuagint, an ancient translation of the Hebrew Scriptures, uses the term "eídō" for "knowing" in the context of this passage. It's more than just intellectual knowledge; it implies experiential understanding, a deep, intimate recognition. By eating the fruit, Adam and Eve were not just gaining information, but a transformative experience that pulled them away from their original nature and design.

Immediately, the repercussions of this trade became evident. They felt shame, a sensation previously unknown in the garden, prompting them to sew fig leaves to cover themselves (Genesis 3:7). Their once-clear vision, unclouded by sin, was now tainted by the knowledge they had traded for. When God called out to them, instead of joyfully running to His presence, they hid in fear.

God, in His omniscience, was fully aware of the trade they had made. Yet, He still approached them, giving them an opportunity to confess. Instead, what followed was a cascade of blame. Adam blamed Eve, and Eve blamed the serpent, highlighting the destructive power of the trade they had initiated.

Their actions ushered in consequences not just for them, but for all of creation. Pain in childbirth, toil in work, and ultimately, physical death became a part of the human experience. Moreover, the spiritual death – the severing of the intimate connection between God and humanity – was the most profound consequence. The ground was cursed because of them, and they were banished from Eden, ensuring that humanity would forever grapple with the repercussions of this inaugural trade.

Adam and Eve's trade with the serpent was not just about a piece of fruit; it was a trade of obedience for autonomy, truth for deception, and life for death. This act has permeated human history, ingraining in us a proclivity to trade, often without fully understanding the consequences.

Through the lens of this foundational narrative, we can begin to discern the patterns of trade in our own lives. The echoes of Eden are found in our daily decisions, as we constantly weigh the value of immediate gratification against eternal significance. The serpent's whisper, questioning God's goodness and intent, still lingers in the recesses of our minds, urging us towards trades that promise freedom but deliver bondage.

Yet, even in the midst of this grim reflection, glimmers of hope emerge. The story of Eden also contains the first prophecy of redemption, where God mentions the seed of the woman who would crush the serpent's head (Genesis 3:15). This veiled reference to Jesus Christ offers a counter-trade: the possibility to trade our brokenness for His wholeness, our sin for His righteousness. It's a reminder that while the inclination to trade may be woven into our nature, the potential for redemption is equally intrinsic, beckoning us towards trades that lead to life and restoration.

In the shadow of the momentous trade made by Adam and Eve, the Bible showcases a tapestry of trades that humanity has engaged in, each teaching us invaluable lessons. From the exchanges between Abraham and Lot to the bartering of Esau's birthright to Jacob, these narratives elucidate the profound consequences of our decisions and the often complex motivations behind them.

Let's consider Abraham and Lot, two kinsmen who journeyed together from their homeland to the Promised Land. As their herds grew, the land could not support both their livestock, leading to disputes between their herdsmen. Abraham, in his wisdom and magnanimity, offered Lot a choice: *"If you go to the left, I'll go to the right; if you go to the right, I'll go to the left"* (Genesis 13:9). Presented with the vast landscapes before him, Lot made a seemingly pragmatic trade. He chose the well-watered plain of the Jordan, which was *"like the garden of the LORD,"* leaving the rugged hills for Abraham. It was a trade of immediate comfort for potential future stability. However, this choice positioned Lot near the wicked cities of Sodom and Gomorrah, leading him into a quagmire of moral corruption and eventual loss. This story starkly portrays how the allure of immediate gains can blind us to long-term consequences.

Similarly, Esau's impulsive trade with Jacob offers profound insights into human nature. Famished from hunting, Esau traded his birthright, a revered spiritual and material inheritance, for a bowl of lentil stew. He declared, *"What good is the birthright to me?"* (Genesis 25:32). The Hebrew word "bekorah," which translates to "birthright," encapsulates not just the material wealth but also the spiritual leadership and blessings of the firstborn. Yet, in his hunger and fatigue, Esau trivialized its importance. The writer of Hebrews later describes Esau as "godless" for this very trade (Hebrews 12:16). Through Esau's shortsightedness, we are reminded of the danger of prioritizing temporary desires over enduring values.

Another compelling example is found in the life of Joseph. Sold into slavery by his envious brothers, Joseph faced a series of trades that tested his character. When Potipar's wife attempted to seduce him, Joseph was presented with a trade: indulge in fleeting pleasure and compromise his integrity or uphold his righteousness and face potential retribution. He chose the latter, declaring, *"How then could I do such a wicked thing and sin against God?"* (Genesis 39:9). Unlike Esau, Joseph recognized the eternal weight of his actions, opting to maintain his relationship with God rather than succumb to immediate temptation.

Yet, it wasn't just the patriarchs who grappled with such decisions. The nation of Israel, throughout its history, was engaged in a series of trades with God. At Mount Sinai, they traded their allegiance to God for a golden calf, leading to severe consequences. Later, during the time of the Judges, they repeatedly traded God's statutes for the practices of the nations around them, leading to cycles of oppression, repentance, and deliverance.

Then, in the days of the prophet Samuel, the Israelites clamored for a king, desiring to be like other nations. They were willing to trade their unique theocratic governance under God for a monarchy that resembled the systems of the world. God, though grieved, granted their request, warning them of the repercussions. This trade led Israel down a tumultuous path, with kings who vacillated between obedience and idolatry.

Delving deeper into the Hebrew context, the word "shamar," meaning "to keep or guard," often appears in the context of Israel's relationship with God's commands. God entrusted His statutes to Israel, expecting them to "shamar" them. However, the frequent trades they made, often for idols and pagan practices, indicate their recurrent failure to guard what was entrusted to them.

In the New Testament, the concept of trade is epitomized in Jesus' poignant question: *"What good will it be for someone to gain the whole world, yet forfeit their soul? Or what can anyone give in exchange for their soul?"* (Matthew 16:26). These words are a stark reminder that the most consequential trades aren't about material gain but are deeply spiritual.

Perhaps one of the most heart-wrenching trades in the New Testament is Judas Iscariot's betrayal of Jesus for thirty pieces of silver. It was a trade of eternal significance for temporal gain, a decision that led to remorse and tragedy. Judas' trade underscores the profound ramifications of prioritizing worldly treasures over spiritual fidelity.

As we traverse these biblical landscapes, we discern a pattern. Time and again, individuals and nations are faced with choices that are, at their core, trades. Some of these trades yield blessings, while others lead to calamity. Whether driven by hunger like Esau, pragmatism like Lot, or integrity like Joseph, these decisions underscore humanity's intrinsic capacity to assess, value, and trade.

Yet, amidst the myriad of trades, a common thread emerges: God's relentless pursuit of a people for Himself. Even when trades led to rebellion and apostasy, God's redemptive plan was undeterred. From the prophecy in Eden of a coming Redeemer to the culmination of that promise in Jesus Christ, God has been orchestrating the most profound trade in history: His righteousness for our sin, His life for our death.

As we reflect on our own lives, we too are confronted with daily trades. The biblical narratives serve as both warnings and encouragements, beckoning us to choose wisely, to prioritize the eternal over the temporal, and to find hope in the ultimate trade offered through Jesus Christ.

CHAPTER 3

Our Personal Trades

Within the intricate tapestry of life, each individual is presented with countless choices, or 'trades' as it were, where decisions must be made, priorities set, and values weighed. The word "trade" evokes images of bartering, of giving one thing in exchange for another. In the spiritual realm, these trades translate to choices that determine what we esteem most, whether it be self-gratification, material gain, or the Kingdom of God.

The Apostle Paul, in his letter to the Philippians, delineates the nature of his personal trades: *"But whatever were gains to me I now consider loss for the sake of Christ. What is more, I consider everything a loss because of the surpassing worth of knowing Christ Jesus my Lord, for whose sake I have lost all things"* (Philippians 3:7-8). Paul's statement wasn't merely poetic or rhetorical; it was rooted in his real-life transformation. Once a respected Pharisee, he traded his status, reputation, and comfort for the sake of the Gospel.

However, not all biblical figures exemplified such selfless trading. The rich young ruler, as depicted in the Gospels, approached Jesus with a query about inheriting eternal life. Jesus' response was challenging: *"Go, sell everything you have and give to the poor, and you will have treasure in heaven. Then come, follow me*" (Mark 10:21). The subsequent narrative is poignant; the young man's face fell, and he left in sorrow. His vast wealth, which he could not part with, represented a trade he wasn't willing to make for the Kingdom of God.

A deeper dive into the original Greek unveils even more nuance. The word "treasure" in the above scripture, "thesauros" in Greek, denotes a place where good and precious things are collected and laid up - a metaphor for the blessings and rewards accrued in Heaven. In a parallel manner, the young ruler had his earthly "thesauros," which he was unwilling to exchange.

Further, Jesus often used parables to depict the Kingdom of God, elucidating the trades made by various characters. The Parable of the Pearl of Great Price in Matthew 13:45-46 is particularly striking. *"Again, the kingdom of heaven is like a merchant seeking fine pearls, and upon finding one pearl of great value, he went and sold all that he had and bought it."* This narrative encapsulates the essence of spiritual trading: recognizing the inestimable value of God's Kingdom and willingly giving up all else to obtain it.

Another illustrative example is found in Luke 14:18-20, where Jesus shares the Parable of the Great Banquet. Invited guests made excuses for not attending the feast. One had purchased a field, another bought oxen, and yet another just got married. Each excuse represents a trade, prioritizing immediate, worldly engagements over a divine invitation.

These parables are not mere allegories but resonate with our daily lives. Each day, we too are presented with choices that mirror these ancient trades. When we opt for a few extra hours of sleep instead of morning prayers, or when earthly pleasures allure us away from spiritual disciplines, we are, in essence, making trades.

Delving into the Hebrew perspective provides more insight. The term "ahav," meaning "to love," is often used to indicate one's ultimate devotion and loyalty. It's the same term used in the paramount commandment: "Love ('ahav') the Lord your God with all your heart and with all your soul and with all your strength" (Deuteronomy 6:5). To love God in this holistic manner means to prioritize Him above all else. However, when other desires occupy this primary space in our hearts, we effectively trade our love for God with love for other things.

The prophet Hosea, through his tumultuous marriage to Gomer, painted a vivid picture of Israel's trades. Just as Gomer frequently traded her marital fidelity for other lovers, Israel repeatedly traded their allegiance to God for foreign idols. Hosea's plea for Israel to return to God serves as a timeless beckon for us to evaluate and rectify the trades we make that displace God from His rightful position in our lives.

The early Christian community in the book of Acts gives us a contrasting picture. They were said to have everything in common, selling their possessions to meet each other's needs (Acts 2:44-45). This was a conscious trade – personal comfort and property for the well-being of the community and the furtherance of God's Kingdom.

Yet, it's essential to recognize that not all personal trades are overt or monumental. More often than not, they are subtle, manifesting in small daily decisions, where the immediate often trumps the eternal. When we prioritize our comfort over compassion, self-interest over service, or materialism over ministry, we trade the eternal riches of God's kingdom for transient worldly gains.

Scripture stands as a testament to both the pitfalls of misguided trades and the blessings of God-centered ones. By revisiting these accounts, we can glean wisdom and find direction for our journey, ensuring that our personal trades align with the eternal values of God's Kingdom.

In the spiritual realm of our lives, the trades we make reflect the deeper yearnings and orientations of our hearts. Jesus, in His profound wisdom, once said, *"For where your treasure is, there your heart will be also"* (Matthew 6:21). This statement is not merely about physical wealth but encompasses the entirety of our desires, priorities, and allegiances.

David, the shepherd-turned-king, is an exemplary figure who often grappled with his desires and allegiances. While he was known as a man after God's own heart, he wasn't without flaw. The incident with Bathsheba is a stark reminder of how even the most spiritually attuned can falter (2 Samuel 11). David, entrapped by his desires, made a series of detrimental trades that started with a mere glance and culminated in deceit, adultery, and even murder. Yet, his subsequent contrition and heartfelt repentance, as captured in Psalm 51, display his deep recognition of the poor trade he had made. *"Create in me a pure heart, O God, and renew a steadfast spirit within me,"* he pleads. This longing to return to a God-centered orientation after a misstep is something every believer can resonate with.

Solomon, David's son, offers another compelling exploration. Gifted with unparalleled wisdom, wealth, and splendor, Solomon had everything one could desire. Yet, in Ecclesiastes, he penned the futility of life's pursuits: *"I have seen all the things that are done under the sun; all of them are meaningless, a chasing after the wind"* (Ecclesiastes 1:14). His introspective reflections come from a place of having made countless trades, many of which, despite their immediate allure, left him feeling empty and unfulfilled. Solomon's words serve as a poignant reminder that not all that glitters is gold, and not every trade that promises joy delivers it.

Drawing from the Greek, the term "kenos," meaning empty or vain, used in the New Testament, particularly encapsulates the essence of Solomon's reflections. Paul, in Philippians 2:7, describes Jesus as taking the form of a servant, being made in human likeness, and *"making himself nothing* (kenos)." Here, the profound trade Christ made is evident. He emptied Himself, set aside His divine prerogatives, and embraced mortality, all for the sake of humanity. In doing so, He demonstrated the ultimate act of selfless trading – prioritizing the salvation of humanity over His divine comfort.

The New Testament also introduces us to Demas, a lesser-known figure who, according to Paul, *"loved this present world"* and consequently deserted the apostolic mission (2 Timothy 4:10). The Greek word for "world" here is "aion," which can be translated to "age," signifying not just the physical world but the prevailing culture, mindset, and temporal values. Demas's trade was choosing the temporal allure of the age over the eternal mission of the Gospel.

Reflecting on such biblical accounts, one might ponder: What drives these trades? At the core, it is the ongoing battle between the flesh and the spirit. Paul eloquently describes this inner tug-of-war in Galatians 5:17: *"For the flesh desires what is contrary to the Spirit, and the Spirit what is contrary to the flesh."* When we operate in the flesh, our trades lean towards immediate gratification, self-promotion, and temporal gains. Conversely, when led by the Spirit, our trades mirror the values of God's Kingdom: love, joy, peace, patience, kindness, goodness, faithfulness, gentleness, and self-control.

Another vivid depiction is found in the story of Mary and Martha (Luke 10:38-42). While Martha busied herself with preparations, arguably important and necessary, Mary chose to sit at Jesus' feet, listening to His teachings. When Martha voiced her frustration, Jesus gently chided her, highlighting that Mary had chosen the better portion. Here, the contrast in their trades is evident: one choosing activity and the other, intimacy with Christ.

From the Hebrew perspective, the term "shalom," often translated as peace, encapsulates a state of wholeness, completeness, and well-being. When our trades are aligned with God's will, they lead us to shalom, a peace that transcends understanding. Yet, misaligned trades disrupt this shalom, leading to turmoil, both internally and externally.

It is crucial, therefore, to continuously assess the trades we make, ensuring they reflect the heart of a Kingdom-seeker. The Apostle James provides a litmus test: *"But the wisdom that comes from heaven is first of all pure; then peace-loving, considerate, submissive, full of mercy and good fruit, impartial and sincere"* (James 3:17). When our trades emanate from this divine wisdom, they invariably lead to fruitful outcomes for God's Kingdom.

In our journey, guided by the Holy Spirit and the wisdom of Scripture, we can navigate the myriad trades presented to us daily, ensuring that our choices honor God and further His Kingdom's purposes on Earth.

CHAPTER 4

Ministry for Whom?

At the very heart of Christian service is the motivation that drives us. Throughout the tapestry of biblical narratives and teachings, we observe this recurring tension between serving for God's glory and seeking human approval. The Bible doesn't shy away from showcasing both commendable examples of servitude and those that serve as cautionary tales.

Paul, in his letters, continually emphasizes the primacy of serving for God's glory. In Galatians 1:10, he asks, *"Am I now trying to win the approval of human beings, or of God? Or am I trying to please people? If I were still trying to please people, I would not be a servant of Christ."* For Paul, this wasn't mere rhetoric. His ministry, fraught with hardship, persecution, and sacrifice, was a testament to his allegiance to Christ over and above any human commendation.

The Apostle's words resonate deeply when we examine the Greek word "doulos," often translated as "servant" or "slave." This term encapsulates complete and utter devotion, without any secondary motives or agendas. In Roman times, a "doulos" was someone who lived solely for the well-being and wishes of their master. For Paul, being a "doulos" of

Christ meant that his ministry was driven by a singular aim: to glorify God, regardless of human opinion.

Yet, the Scriptures also present characters who grappled with the allure of human approval. The Pharisees, the religious elite of Jesus' time, often fall into this category. Jesus chastised them, saying, *"Everything they do is done for people to see"* (Matthew 23:5). Their piety, while seemingly impeccable on the outside, was tainted by the desire for human accolades. They loved "the place of honor at banquets and the most important seats in the synagogues; to be greeted with respect in the marketplaces and to be called 'Rabbi' by others" (Matthew 23:6-7).

A deep dive into Hebrew provides further insight. The word "kavod" is often translated as "glory" or "honor." In its original essence, it carries a weightiness or heaviness. When the Old Testament speaks of God's "kavod," it refers to His divine weightiness, majesty, and the due recognition He deserves. Conversely, when humans seek "kavod" for themselves, it signifies a misplaced desire for weightiness or importance in the eyes of others.

King Saul's trajectory is an illustrative example. Initially chosen by God and anointed by Samuel, Saul began his reign with humility. However, as time progressed, the weight of leadership and the lure of human approval skewed his priorities. His incomplete obedience in the battle against the Amalekites, sparing King Agag and the best livestock, was a pivotal moment (1 Samuel 15). When confronted by Samuel, Saul's response was telling: *"I feared the people and so I gave in to them"* (1 Samuel 15:24). Saul's admission lays bare a challenge many face: the fear of man superseding the fear of God.

In contrast, John the Baptist stands as a beacon of selfless ministry. Aware of his role as the forerunner to the Messiah, he declared,

"He must increase, but I must decrease" (John 3:30). The Greek term "auxano," translated as "increase," conveys growth, advancement, or magnification. John's ministry wasn't about his own elevation but about magnifying Christ. Even as crowds flocked to him, he remained unwavering in pointing them to Jesus, the Lamb of God.

This struggle isn't limited to biblical times. Contemporary ministry, with the advent of technology and social media, presents myriad avenues for acclaim and recognition. Pastors, evangelists, and Christian influencers can amass followers, likes, and shares, blurring the lines between genuine service for God's glory and subtle (or not-so-subtle) self-promotion.

Paul offers timeless wisdom in this regard: *"Whatever you do, do it all for the glory of God"* (1 Corinthians 10:31). The Greek word "doxa," from which "glory" is derived, encompasses splendor, brightness, and magnificence. When ministry is rooted in seeking God's "doxa," it shines brightly, reflecting His magnificence to a world in need of His light.

Yet, the journey to such a ministry isn't without its challenges. As servants of Christ, we must consistently examine our motives, realigning ourselves with the call to serve selflessly. Through prayer, introspection, and godly counsel, we can navigate the nuanced path of ministry, ensuring that it remains, above all, for the "doxa" of God.

In understanding the nature of ministry, we are consistently called back to the teachings of Jesus Himself. The Savior's life exemplified an unparalleled model of selfless service, often rebuking the self-righteous and prideful. He, who was without sin, perfectly exemplified how ministry should be anchored.

When the mother of James and John requested places of honor for her sons in Jesus' kingdom, the reaction of the other disciples was one of indignation. They too harbored aspirations of greatness and esteem. But Jesus' response to them was a revolutionary definition of leadership and service: *"You know that the rulers of the Gentiles lord it over them, and their great ones exercise authority over them. It shall not be so among you. But whoever would be great among you must be your servant, and whoever would be first among you must be your slave, even as the Son of Man came not to be served but to serve, and to give his life as a ransom for many"* (Matthew 20:25-28).

Diving deeper into the Greek, the word "diakonos" is used for "servant", which means "attendant" or "waiter". From this term, we get the word "deacon", a role within many Christian denominations characterized by service. Jesus radically proposes that true greatness in the Kingdom of God is defined not by how many serve you, but by how many you serve.

The Hebrew Bible offers us another profound instance with the life of David. While Saul's downfall was expedited by his hunger for approval, David, despite his flaws, was described as *"a man after God's own heart."* But why? David had his share of failures and sins, but his heart was consistently turned towards repentance and reliance on God. After his grievous sin with Bathsheba, David's plea in Psalm 51:10 was, *"Create in me a pure heart, O God, and renew a steadfast spirit within me."* His primary concern was the restoration of his relationship with God, not merely the preservation of his kingship or reputation. David recognized that the real audience for his life and kingship wasn't the masses or even his royal court, but God Himself.

This dichotomy of serving God versus seeking human approval isn't solely an external battle; it's deeply internal. The human heart, with its intricacies and desires, often leans towards recognition and approval. Jeremiah 17:9 warns, *"The heart is deceitful above all things and beyond cure."* This pronouncement might sound dire, but it's a necessary reminder. Without vigilance, even the most devout can fall prey to the seduction of accolades.

The Apostle Peter, known for his impulsive nature, offers a transformative example. At one moment, he's declaring his unwavering loyalty to Jesus, and in the next, he denies Him thrice. However, post-resurrection, Peter's encounter with Jesus on the shores of the Sea of Tiberias marked a turning point. Jesus' threefold question, *"Do you love me?" followed by the command "Feed my sheep,"* (John 21:15-17) was more than just a restoration of Peter. It was a recalibration of his ministry's focus. Love for Jesus was to be the cornerstone, and from that foundation, service would flow.

Paul, in his second letter to the Corinthians, speaks of the *"thorn in the flesh"* (2 Corinthians 12:7). While the exact nature of this "thorn" remains a subject of theological debate, Paul's response to it is instructive. He prayed for its removal, but God's response was, *"My grace is sufficient for you, for my power is made perfect in weakness."* The Apostle's realization was profound: *"Therefore I will boast all the more gladly of my weaknesses, so that the power of Christ may rest upon me."*

Paul's approach serves as a poignant lesson for modern ministry. In acknowledging weaknesses, imperfections, and utter dependence on God's grace, ministers can deflect human praise. It's no longer about the eloquence of a sermon, the success of a church program, or the reach of an evangelistic campaign. It becomes about the transformative power of Christ working through fallible human vessels.

In every era, the trappings of recognition beckon – whether it's the chief seats in synagogues of yesteryears, or the viral videos and massive followership of today's digital age. The question that every minister must grapple with remains: For whom am I doing this?

The Apostle James offers a fitting exhortation, "Humble yourselves before the Lord, and he will lift you up" (James 4:10). The Greek verb "tapeinóō", translated as "humble", means to bring low or to be ranked beneath. It's a call to recognize one's position in relation to the Almighty. When this perspective is clear, the allure of human praise dims in the overwhelming light of God's glory.

Ministry is a high calling, one that demands continuous introspection and alignment with God's will. While the world may chant praises or hurl criticisms, the minister's ear must be attuned to the gentle whisper of the Divine, guiding, correcting, and affirming. In this sacred endeavor, seeking God's glory becomes the only approval worth pursuing.

CHAPTER 5

Righteousness Redefined

The concept of righteousness is central to the Judeo-Christian ethos. Throughout the Hebrew Bible, righteousness was often linked with adherence to the Law. But with the coming of Jesus Christ, there was a profound shift in understanding. Jesus, during His earthly ministry, radically redefined righteousness, focusing less on mere external compliance and more on the inner motives and inclinations of the heart.

To understand this transformation, one must first grasp the original concept of righteousness. In the Hebrew Bible, the term often used for righteousness is "tsedeq." Rooted in the idea of justice, it implies a conformity to a moral standard, often encapsulated in the Mosaic Law. Observing the Sabbath, offering correct sacrifices, and maintaining ceremonial cleanliness were all key components of this understanding.

Yet, when Jesus began His public ministry, He confronted this external-centric view head-on. The Sermon on the Mount, found in Matthew chapters 5 through 7, serves as the most comprehensive discourse on this subject. Here, Jesus took the established norms of righteousness and deepened them, introducing a heart-centric paradigm.

He begins with what seems like a startling statement: *"For I tell you, unless your righteousness exceeds that of the scribes and Pharisees, you will never enter the kingdom of heaven"* (Matthew 5:20). Given that the Pharisees were considered paragons of piety, this statement was radical. Yet, as He elucidated, the nature of His assertion became clear.

Take, for instance, His commentary on murder: *"You have heard that it was said to those of old, 'You shall not murder; and whoever murders will be liable to judgment.' But I say to you that everyone who is angry with his brother will be liable to judgment"* (Matthew 5:21-22). Here, Jesus elevates the standard from the physical act of murder to the internal emotion of anger.

The Greek term used for "angry" here is "orgizó," which means to provoke or enrage. Jesus emphasizes that harboring such feelings is as grave as the act of murder itself. The focus shifts from mere actions to the motives and feelings behind them.

In a similar vein, He addresses adultery: *"You have heard that it was said, 'You shall not commit adultery.' But I say to you that everyone who looks at a woman with lustful intent has already committed adultery with her in his heart"* (Matthew 5:27-28). Here, the term "lustful intent" translates from the Greek "epithumeó," which means to desire or covet. Once again, Jesus moves the focus inward, emphasizing the importance of purity in thought and intent, not just in action.

Such teachings brought a seismic shift in the Jewish understanding of righteousness. For centuries, the emphasis had largely been on external observances. Jesus, however, was spotlighting a deeper, more profound reality: that true righteousness starts from the heart and then manifests in actions. It wasn't enough to avoid committing a sin in the physical realm; one had to guard against it in the spiritual realm of thoughts and emotions as well.

Jesus also pointed out the pitfalls of performative righteousness, wherein acts of piety were done primarily for public recognition. He critiqued such displays, saying, "*And when you pray, you must not be like the hypocrites. For they love to stand and pray in the synagogues and at the street corners, that they may be seen by others*" (Matthew 6:5). The Greek term "hypokrités," translated as "hypocrites," originally referred to actors on a stage. Jesus was highlighting the danger of making righteousness a performance rather than a sincere, heart-driven endeavor.

Additionally, Jesus' interactions with individuals underscored this theme. When He met the rich young ruler, despite the latter's impeccable adherence to the Law, Jesus pinpointed his heart's attachment to wealth (Mark 10:17-22). Or consider His conversation with the Samaritan woman, where He transcended the external improprieties of her life to address the deeper thirst of her soul (John 4:7-26).

In redefining r ighteousness, Jesus was not n ullifying t he Law but fulfilling it. He was calling humanity to a higher standard, one that was less about checkboxes of do's and don'ts and more about genuine transformation from the inside out.

The Apostle Paul, in his epistles, expanded on this theme. He wrote about the futility of seeking righteousness through the Law alone and emphasized the need for inner transformation through Christ (Romans 3:20-22). The Greek term "dikaiosynē," commonly translated as righteousness in Paul's letters, encapsulates this idea of being in right standing—not by mere actions, but by faith and heart alignment with God.

Thus, Jesus' teaching on righteousness was revolutionary. It challenged the status quo and upended traditional paradigms. It shifted the focus from hands to heart, from actions to intentions, and from rituals to relationships. In His call to a deeper, more genuine righteousness, Jesus beckoned humanity to an intimate, transformative relationship with the Divine—a call that echoes through the ages, as relevant today as it was two millennia ago.

As the teachings of Jesus swept through the nascent Christian communities, they ignited both a sense of awe and discomfort. The redefined standard of righteousness was not just a theological novelty; it was a call to introspection, an invitation to peer into the soul's depths and reassess one's relationship with God.

The Pharisees, for all their stringency in upholding the Law, were often chided by Jesus. Why? Because their rigorous external observances were bereft of love, humility, and mercy – values that Jesus posited at the core of true righteousness. This dynamic is most starkly illustrated in His parable of the Pharisee and the Tax Collector. "Two men went up into the temple to pray, one a Pharisee and the other a tax collector. The Pharisee, standing by himself, prayed thus: 'God, I thank you that I am not like other men, extortioners, unjust, adulterers, or even like this tax collector. I fast twice a week; I give tithes of all that I get.' But the tax collector, standing far off, would not even lift up his eyes to heaven, but beat his breast, saying, *'God, be merciful to me, a sinner!' I tell you, this man went down to his house justified, rather than the other"* (Luke 18:10-14).

The Pharisee, in this parable, exemplifies the danger of self-righteousness. His prayer is replete with self-congratulation, and there's an absence of humility. The Greek word for justified, "dikaioō", means to be declared righteous. This tax collector, despite his societal image and past, was deemed righteous by God because of his genuine contrition and humility, not because of a litany of good deeds.

Jesus consistently emphasized the value of the heart's condition over external manifestations. The Greek word "kardia" translates to "heart" in English and denotes one's innermost being, the hub of personal desires, and emotions. The heart's purity and intent were paramount. As He said, *"Blessed are the pure in heart, for they shall see God"* (Matthew 5:8).

But how does one cultivate such purity in heart? It's not about renouncing actions but reorienting them. Jesus' teachings highlight the significance of intentions. Acts of charity, for example, should emanate from genuine compassion, not a desire for praise. Prayer should be a heartfelt dialogue with God, not an ostentatious display. Righteousness, then, is not about abolishing actions but refining motives.

The Apostle James, in his epistle, aptly encapsulated this synergy between faith (heart beliefs) and works (actions). *"What good is it, my brothers, if someone says he has faith but does not have works? Can that faith save him?"* (James 2:14). James wasn't contradicting the Pauline doctrine of justification by faith; rather, he was emphasizing that authentic faith inevitably manifests in righteous deeds.

For early Christians, this heart-centric righteousness also had social implications. It wasn't just about personal piety; it impacted how they engaged with society. The Apostle John writes, *"But if anyone has the world's goods and sees his brother in need, yet closes his heart against him, how does God's love abide in him?"* (1 John 3:17). The Greek term "splanchnizomai", often used in the New Testament, means to feel compassion. It indicates a visceral, deep-seated emotion. True righteousness, then, compels action, especially in the face of suffering and need.

In the Hebrew Bible, the term "chesed" often appears, typically translated as "lovingkindness" or "steadfast love." This word carries connotations of loyalty, faithfulness, and mercy. Righteousness, in the holistic biblical sense, is intrinsically tied to "chesed." It's not just about personal purity but also about extending God's lovingkindness to others.

One profound biblical account that embodies this redefined righteousness is the story of the Good Samaritan (Luke 10:25-37). In this parable, a man, presumably Jewish, is left for dead by robbers. While religious leaders pass by, it is a Samaritan, historically seen as an adversary of the Jews, who showcases genuine righteousness by caring for the injured man. Jesus used this parable not just to redefine neighborliness but also to underscore that true righteousness transcends religious and ethnic boundaries.

By spotlighting the Samaritan's acts, Jesus challenged the established norms of societal righteousness. He presented a model where mercy, compassion, and selfless love were the true markers of righteousness, not just religious pedigree or ethnic identity.

Such narratives invite introspection. They prompt believers to assess the authenticity of their righteousness. Are one's deeds motivated by love and humility, or are they tainted by pride and self-seeking? Does one's righteousness extend beyond personal piety to encompass societal engagement, especially towards the marginalized and oppressed?

In redefining righteousness, Jesus was inviting humanity to a richer, fuller relationship with God—a relationship rooted in love, humility, and authentic transformation. Such righteousness isn't merely about avoiding wrong actions; it's about cultivating right affections—those that align with the heart of God. This remains a poignant call, echoing through the corridors of time, urging believers toward a deeper, genuine walk with the Divine.

CHAPTER 6

Demonic Influences

In the complex tapestry of human experience, wisdom is a cherished virtue, often sought after and revered. Yet, the Bible speaks of wisdom that comes from above and wisdom that is earthly, unspiritual, even demonic. It's crucial to understand the nature and consequences of these forms of wisdom, for they shape our decisions, interactions, and most importantly, our spiritual trades.

The Apostle James, in his epistle, delineates between these sources of wisdom. *"Who is wise and understanding among you? Let them show it by their good life, by deeds done in the humility that comes from wisdom. But if you harbor bitter envy and selfish ambition in your hearts, do not boast about it or deny the truth. Such 'wisdom' does not come down from heaven but is earthly, unspiritual, demonic. For where you have envy and selfish ambition, there you find disorder and every evil practice. But the wisdom that comes from heaven is first of all pure; then peace-loving, considerate, submissive, full of mercy and good fruit, impartial and sincere"* (James 3:13-17).

Here, James contrasts two wisdom types. The first, driven by envy and ambition, results in strife and evil practices. The Greek word for envy, "zelos", can imply fervor or jealousy, and the term for selfish ambition, "eritheia", suggests faction or contention. Such attitudes lead to "akatastasia", meaning instability or disorder.

On the other hand, divine wisdom promotes purity, peace, mercy, and sincerity. It's evident that these wisdom forms yield different fruit and subsequently different outcomes in our spiritual trading.

It's pertinent to examine one of the most profound trades in biblical history involving earthly and demonic wisdom: The Fall. In the Garden of Eden, Satan, as the serpent, used crafty words to deceive Eve. *"Did God really say, 'You must not eat from any tree in the garden'?"* (Genesis 3:1). Here, the enemy did not just question God's command but subtly cast doubts on His character and intentions.

Eve's trade with the serpent wasn't just about a fruit; it was an exchange of divine wisdom for earthly wisdom. The moment she considered the fruit "desirable for gaining wisdom", she traded divine revelation for earthly reasoning, a transaction that led humanity into sin and separation from God.

The Hebrew term for wisdom, "chokmah", implies skill in living, but it's essential to discern whose skillset we're applying: God's or the world's. For Eve, the enticement of becoming *"like God"* (Genesis 3:5) overshadowed the established divine wisdom. This first trade, influenced by demonic persuasion, set a precedent for the dangers of yielding to ungodly wisdom.

Furthermore, the New Testament repeatedly warns believers about the perils of deceptive philosophies and traditions. The Apostle Paul, writing to the Colossians, states, *"See to it that no one takes you captive by philosophy and empty deceit, according to human tradition, according to the elemental spirits of the world, and not according to Christ"* (Colossians

2:8). The Greek term "stoicheion" translates to "elemental spirits", suggesting foundational principles or elemental forces of the world, which can be influenced by demonic realms.

One of the most poignant biblical illustrations of the consequences of yielding to demonic wisdom is King Saul. Initially anointed by God, Saul started well but gradually gave in to impatience, jealousy, and disobedience. The tragic narrative in 1 Samuel 28 depicts Saul consulting a medium, seeking guidance from the deceased prophet Samuel. This act of necromancy, strictly forbidden by Mosaic Law, was Saul's desperate trade, choosing demonic counsel over waiting on God's direction. Such a decision only expedited his downfall.

In our lives, these trades might not be as dramatic as Eve's or Saul's, but the subtleties can be equally, if not more, treacherous. Whether it's prioritizing cultural norms over biblical truths, seeking success at the expense of integrity, or allowing fear and insecurity to dictate our decisions—these are all instances of trading divine wisdom for earthly or demonic influences.

How then do we guard against such deceptive trades? The Psalmist offers a solution: *"Your word is a lamp to my feet and a light to my path"* (Psalm 119:105). Immersing oneself in God's Word, seeking His wisdom, and cultivating discernment through the Holy Spirit are paramount.

Recognizing and resisting demonic influences is essential in our spiritual journey. While the wisdom of the world can be enticing, offering immediate gains or solutions, it often leads to spiritual deficits. As believers, our challenge is to continuously evaluate the trades we make, ensuring they are anchored in God's wisdom and not influenced by earthly or demonic persuasions.

In our exploration of demonic influences and the ensuing consequences, one might wonder: why is such wisdom so tempting? Why, despite the inherent dangers, do people—both in biblical times and today—find themselves drawn to the allure of earthly and demonic wisdom? The answer lies in the human heart's intricacies and the immediate, yet fleeting, rewards these forms of wisdom seem to offer.

To understand this allure, we should turn to the story of King Solomon, widely celebrated for his unparalleled wisdom. Solomon's prayer for understanding and discernment pleased God, and the Lord endowed him with wisdom like no other (1 Kings 3:12). Yet, even Solomon, with all his divine insight, fell prey to influences that ultimately led him astray.

The scripture recounts how Solomon's foreign wives turned his heart after other gods, leading him into idolatry (1 Kings 11:4). How could a man so discerning, who wrote extensive proverbs and gave counsel to kings from distant lands, deviate so profoundly? The allure of foreign alliances, political power, and perhaps the cultural luxuries of his wives' nations enticed Solomon. Here, the wisdom of worldly diplomacy and short-term gains traded off with the enduring wisdom of God's commands.

The Greek word "sophia" is often translated as wisdom. Still, it's essential to note that it doesn't merely denote intellectual understanding. It encapsulates broader concepts of insight, skill, and expertise in varied arts. Solomon's diverse pursuits—whether in architecture, commerce, or the arts—exemplify this multi-faceted wisdom. Yet, the divergence from God's ways showcases how even such expansive knowledge can be misdirected when not rooted in reverence for the Almighty.

The New Testament brings this point home more explicitly. In his letter to the Romans, Paul presents a biting critique of those who, despite claiming wisdom, became fools by turning away from the Creator to worship creation (Romans 1:22-23). The term "moria," from which the English word "moron" is derived, is used in the original Greek text to denote the folly of such a choice. The irony couldn't be starker: in seeking wisdom apart from God, humanity descends into the deepest folly.

But what's the lure? Why do these forms of wisdom, even when ungodly, seem so appealing? One factor is the immediate gratification they seem to offer. Earthly wisdom often promises quick fixes, tangible rewards, or social accolades. Similarly, demonic influences, while inherently malevolent, can masquerade as benign or even beneficial. The Apostle Paul cautions that Satan himself can transform into an angel of light (2 Corinthians 11:14). This masquerade makes discerning such influences even more challenging.

Another reason is the innate human desire for autonomy. Just as Eve was enticed by the prospect of becoming *"like God,"* there's a deep-seated inclination in humanity to be in control, to be the masters of their destiny, even if it means sidelining the Creator. This quest for self-rule, fueled by earthly and demonic wisdom, often seems more attractive than the path of submission and obedience to God.

It's also worth noting that the environment and societal structures play a role. Just as Solomon's alliances influenced his spiritual fidelity, the societies and cultures we inhabit can sway our understanding of wisdom. The Hebrew word "sekel," another term for wisdom, can also imply prudence or circumspection. In a world brimming with myriad influences, exercising such circumspection becomes vital.

Yet, even in the midst of these challenges, the Bible offers hope and guidance. James, the half-brother of Jesus, provides a clear antidote: *"If any of you lacks wisdom, you should ask God, who gives generously to all without finding fault, and it will be given to you"* (James 1:5). This divine wisdom, grounded in the fear of the Lord, serves as a bulwark against the pull of earthly and demonic influences.

Moreover, the Holy Spirit's role as the Spirit of Truth aids believers in discerning and navigating the myriad voices clamoring for attention. Jesus, in his farewell discourse, assures His disciples that the Advocate will guide them into all truth (John 16:13). Through the Spirit's indwelling, believers are equipped to discern, resist, and overcome the snares of false wisdom.

In reflecting upon the choices and trades made by biblical figures and the exhortations of the apostles, it becomes clear that the battle for true wisdom is both arduous and relentless. Yet, the stakes couldn't be higher. The trades we make, whether influenced by divine wisdom or its counterfeit forms, have eternal implications. It's a challenge, then, to continually anchor oneself in God's Word, seek His face, and rely on the Spirit's guidance, ensuring that our trades lead us closer to the heart of God rather than away from it.

CHAPTER 7

The Journey Begins

From the vibrant tapestries of biblical narratives to the lived experiences of believers throughout history, the concept of trading, in its spiritual sense, emerges as a universal truth. Every soul, knowingly or unknowingly, stands at the trading floors of decision, bargaining the present for the future, the tangible for the earthly, and, more touchingly, the temporal for the eternal.

As is the case with many profound revelations, the understanding of these spiritual trades came to me not in the serenity of a mountaintop but amid the tumultuous valleys of personal struggles and confrontations. My story is one marked by resistance, reckoning, and ultimately, redemption. It's the tale of a boy who grew weary of church's wooden benches, only to realize years later that the problem wasn't the pew but the posture of his heart.

My early years were steeped in church culture. Sundays meant starched shirts, gleaming shoes, and long hours listening to sermons that, to my young ears, seemed as endless as they were esoteric. My mother, a stalwart of faith, believed in the redemptive power of church attendance. Her devotion was unwavering, a constant that mirrored the Old Testament

Israelites' steadfast adherence to the law. The Hebrew word "qum," meaning "to arise" or "stand," perhaps best captures her tenacity. Come rain or shine, in seasons of joy or in the shadow of grief, we were in church. And while her intent was pure, the relentless routine fostered in me a growing resentment.

"I'll never step into a church once I'm out on my own," I'd often declare, the adolescent rebellion in my voice unmistakable. As the years rolled by, this sentiment grew stronger. The ancient Greeks had a word, "apostasia," which means a "falling away" or "defection." Originally, it wasn't laden with the theological implications it carries today. However, in my journey, it mirrored the gradual distancing from God's house and, more critically, from His presence.

True to my word, adulthood brought with it the autonomy I had so fervently desired. Freed from my mother's watchful gaze and the church's perceived shackles, I indulged in a life I thought was my own making. But with every decision, every trade I made on the floors of ambition, pleasure, and pride, I was unknowingly bartering pieces of my soul.

It's a subtle, almost imperceptible transaction. One doesn't immediately sense the loss, much like Esau, who for a single meal traded his birthright (Genesis 25:29-34). The gratification of the immediate blinds one to the eternal ramifications. The Greek word "parallage," meaning "exchange" or "alteration," aptly describes this dynamic. The choices I made, the priorities I set, they all seemed justified in the moment, but they were shifting the very core of my being, exchanging eternal truths for fleeting falsehoods.

One evening, in the quiet solitude of my thoughts, a revelation struck me. It wasn't accompanied by thunderclaps or divine apparitions but was a gentle, persistent nudging of the spirit. The trading floors. The very concept that I had been exploring academically and theoretically was playing out in my life, not in abstract theology but in concrete choices.

I recalled the parable of the Prodigal Son, a narrative I had heard countless times from the church pulpit. The younger son, restless and eager for autonomy, demanded his inheritance and set off to distant lands, seeking pleasure and prosperity. However, when famine struck and he found himself destitute, he realized the gravity of his trades. He had exchanged the warmth of his father's house for the cold embrace of a pigsty.

This parable, as told in Luke 15:11-32, wasn't just a tale from ancient times. It was my story. The allure of worldly wisdom, the siren call of autonomy, had led me away from the Father's house. But that evening's revelation was not one of despair. It was a beckoning, an invitation to return, to repent.

The Greek term "metanoia," often translated as repentance, carries with it the idea of a change of mind, a transformative rethinking of one's life. It's not just about feeling sorry but about turning around, heading in a new direction. That night, I began my journey of metanoia.

In the days and months that followed, the trading floors took on a new meaning. They were no longer just spaces of commerce but arenas of the soul, where daily decisions held eternal significance. The trades I had made, choices that had led me away from God's presence, came into sharp focus.

But this journey was not one of self-flagellation or miserable introspection. It was a pilgrimage of grace. Just as the Prodigal Son's father ran to him, embracing him with love and forgiveness, I felt God's encompassing grace drawing me back. The Hebrew term "chesed," often translated as "loving-kindness" or "steadfast love," became a lived reality. Despite my trades, my poor decisions, the Father's chesed remained unwavering.

The story of my return to God's embrace, to the true understanding of the trading floors of life, is one of profound gratitude. It's a testament to God's relentless pursuit of the lost, His yearning to restore and redeem. Every soul, no matter how distant or disillusioned, is invited to this journey, to recognize the trades, repent, and return to the loving arms of the Father. The journey, as I came to realize, is not about reaching a destination but about recognizing who we're journeying with.

As I continued along the path of rediscovery and reconnection, I realized that God's interventions in our lives are not confined to a single, definitive moment. Instead, they sprawl across our journey, manifesting in unexpected times and places, ushering in profound transformations. One such epiphanic moment transpired on an otherwise ordinary Saturday morning.

Riding to work, my truck radio seemed to have developed a mind of its own, landing me on a channel I didn't recognize. The deep, resonant voice of Adrian Rogers filled the confines of my car. At that moment, I wasn't just another listener in a vast audience. It felt as if he was speaking directly, solely to me.

"You think you have it all together," he began, his voice a blend of compassion and authority. "The house, the picket fence, the dog, the wife. But you have nothing—absolutely nothing—if you don't have Jesus."

His words bore into my very soul. The worldly trading floors, where I had bartered happiness for possessions and spiritual wealth for fleeting pleasures, came flooding back. All those trades seemed hollow, pale in comparison to the eternal wealth and joy that come from knowing Jesus.

And then, in a moment that felt suspended in time, Adrian Rogers invited his listeners to pray with him. "Repeat after me," he prompted. And as he prayed, I echoed, every word reverberating deep within my spirit. It wasn't just the utterance of words; it was a deep-seated proclamation, a soulful pledge. Something indescribable shifted within me. The very core of my being experienced a transformation, as if scales had fallen from my eyes, revealing a world of spiritual truth and clarity.

Overwhelmed by emotion and the gravity of the moment, I began discarding my worldly CDs, one by one, out of the car window. Each disc represented not just music but a part of my past, a segment of the old trading floor that had kept me ensnared in worldly trappings. With tears streaming down my face, it wasn't just about letting go of material possessions but also about releasing old burdens, regrets, and the weight of decisions that had kept me from God's perfect plan.

This newfound freedom was exhilarating. Yet, the journey with God is not one of perpetual highs. There are valleys, moments of weakness where old habits beckon and the lure of former trading floors tempts. To claim otherwise would be disingenuous. Indeed, the Apostle John wrote in his first epistle, *"If we claim to be without sin, we deceive ourselves and the truth is not in us"* (1 John 1:8). Every believer, no matter how mature or devout, grapples with this human condition. We sometimes find ourselves trading on the other side, making choices that don't align with our heavenly calling.

Yet, in these moments of frailty, a beautiful truth emerges: GRACE. The Greek word "charis" embodies this concept of grace. It's an unmerited favor, a divine assistance given to humans for their regeneration or sanctification. Even when we falter, even when we revisit old trading floors, God's grace remains abundant, ready to pull us back into His embrace.

This grace is not an excuse to continue in our old ways, but a lifeline, a reminder of God's unwavering love and commitment to our journey. The Apostle Paul reminds us in Romans 5:20, *"Where sin increased, grace increased all the more."* This isn't a call to complacency but a testament to the boundless nature of God's grace. It's a promise that no matter how many times we find ourselves on the wrong trading floor, His hand is always extended, ready to guide us back.

My encounter with Adrian Rogers on that fateful Saturday morning was not just a turning point but a testament to God's continual pursuit. God uses various channels, moments, and messengers to draw us closer to Him. It's a dynamic, ever-evolving relationship where every day offers a new opportunity to trade our will for His, our plans for His divine purpose.

And as I journey forward, I am continually reminded of the vastness of God's grace, the beauty of His redemption, and the transformative power of His love. Each day presents its challenges, its trading floors, but with God by my side, I am learning to make trades that echo into eternity.

CHAPTER 8

Floor One – Tyre:

The ancient city of Tyre, once a bustling port and trading hub, serves as an evocative backdrop to understanding the spiritual implications of money and materialism in our lives. Set against the shimmering blue of the Mediterranean, Tyre thrived on its robust trade, establishing itself as one of the greatest merchant cities in antiquity. Yet, the Scriptures offer more than just a historical account of its commerce. Tyre becomes emblematic of the allure of worldly riches and the inherent dangers when they eclipse divine purpose.

The prophet Ezekiel provides one of the most vivid descriptions of Tyre's grandeur and subsequent judgment. In Ezekiel 28:12-17, the King of Tyre is addressed, but the undertones hint at a deeper, spiritual entity, possibly Satan: *"You were the seal of perfection, full of wisdom and perfect in beauty... Every precious stone adorned you... Your settings and mountings were made of gold... You were on the holy mount of God... Till wickedness was found in you."* While the primary interpretation pertains to Tyre's king, the passage is believed by many scholars to allude to Lucifer's initial beauty and his eventual fall.

This imagery intertwines Tyre's material prosperity with spiritual pride. The Hebrew term "ruwm" can be translated to "exalt" or "lift up." This lifting up of oneself, fueled by the riches of the world, becomes a precarious pedestal. For Tyre, its unmatched wealth was not merely a source of pride but became the very essence of its identity, overshadowing any acknowledgment of God's providence. This over-reliance and obsession with material wealth is an ancient manifestation of a challenge that remains relevant even today.

To fully grasp the spiritual implications of Tyre's trading floor, one must understand the sheer scope of its commerce. Ships from Tarshish, distant lands, and various islands flocked to its ports. Silver, iron, tin, lead, garments, wines, and a plethora of other commodities were traded, making Tyre an epitome of wealth (Ezekiel 27:12-24). But it's not just the tangible goods that matter. The Greek term "kērygma" means proclamation or heralding. Tyre's unmatched wealth wasn't silent; it heralded a kērygma of self-sufficiency and grandeur, often sidelining any divine narrative.

This trading floor of materialism extends beyond Tyre's ancient walls to our modern lives. In a world where one's worth is often measured by bank balances and material acquisitions, the whisperings of Tyre echo louder than ever. Money and possessions, inherently neutral, can, when misplaced, become tools of pride, self-sufficiency, and a departure from God's guidance.

Jesus, during His ministry, frequently touched upon the theme of wealth and its potential pitfalls. *"Do not lay up for yourselves treasures on earth... but lay up for yourselves treasures in heaven... For where your treasure is, there your heart will be also"* (Matthew 6:19-21). The Greek word "thēsauros" denotes a place where good and precious things are collected and laid up, a treasure chest. Jesus's admonition to prioritize heavenly thēsauros over earthly ones underscores the transient nature of material wealth.

Yet, understanding this doesn't necessitate an ascetic life. The intent isn't to shun money or label it inherently evil. Instead, the Biblical narrative encourages a balanced perspective. When Apostle Paul writes to Timothy, he mentions, *"For the love of money is a root of all kinds of evil"* (1 Timothy 6:10). It's the "love" of money, not money itself, that poses the danger. The Greek term "philargyria" literally translates to "a fondness of silver" or "avarice." It's this excessive attachment, this philargyria, that Paul cautions against.

Tyre's trading floor serves as a cautionary tale. It invites introspection: What treasures dominate our hearts? Are we treading the bustling markets of Tyre, ensnared by the glitter of gold and silver, or are we navigating our lives with an eternal perspective, seeking treasures that rust and moth cannot destroy?

As we delve deeper into understanding the spiritual floors of trade in subsequent chapters, Tyre's legacy serves as a foundation. It reminds us of the ephemeral nature of worldly wealth and the eternal significance of where we lay our treasures. In the words of the Psalmist, *"If riches increase, set not your heart upon them"* (Psalm 62:10). It's this balance, this divine perspective on material wealth, that Tyre beckons us to discover.

As we further immerse ourselves in Tyre's tale, it's essential to recognize the intrinsic connection between materialism and the human heart. This isn't a story confined to ancient history. The resonance of Tyre's trading floors reverberates through the centuries, manifesting in our modern age with startling clarity.

Tyre was more than just a prosperous city; it became a symbol of opulence, ambition, and worldly success. But intertwined with its tale is a spiritual lesson on the perils of misplaced devotion. In ancient times, every significant city had its patron deity, its "god" that supposedly brought it protection and prosperity. For Tyre, that deity was Melqart, often equated with the legendary Hercules. The people believed that their city's prosperity was tied to Melqart's favor. Consequently, their devotion was split, with God being sidelined.

This spiritual dynamic is reflected in the word "avad," a Hebrew term which can mean "to work," "to serve," or even "to worship." In essence, what one works for, or where one invests effort and resources, becomes the object of worship. Tyre's inhabitants worked tirelessly for material gain, and in doing so, their service to Melqart, their god of prosperity, intensified.

James, in his epistle, touches upon a similar dynamic: *"You adulterous people! Do you not know that friendship with the world is enmity with God? Therefore, whoever wishes to be a friend of the world makes himself an enemy of God"* (James 4:4). The Greek term "moichalís," translated as "adulterous," suggests unfaithfulness, much like a spouse being unfaithful in a marriage. By seeking friendship and approval from the world and its materialistic values, believers risk distancing themselves from God.

This dynamic presents a challenging question for modern believers: In our pursuit of success, have we inadvertently set up altars to gods of wealth, status, and materialism? Just as Tyre's prosperity was both its strength and its potential downfall, the treasures we chase today can ensnare our hearts, diverting our focus from the eternal to the temporal.

Jesus once encountered a man who provides a stark example of this dynamic. Known as the rich young ruler, this man approached Jesus with a question about eternal life. As their conversation unfolded, Jesus discerned the man's heart's true attachment: *"If you want to be perfect, go, sell your possessions and give to the poor, and you will have treasure in heaven. Then come, follow me."* The man's reaction was telling; he went away sad because he had great wealth (Matthew 19:16-22).

In the Greek text, the term "lypeō" is used to describe the man's reaction, which translates to "grieve" or "be sorrowful." His heart was bound to his possessions, revealing where his true devotion lay. Like the inhabitants of Tyre, the rich young ruler was ensnared by his material blessings, unable to see beyond them to the greater treasure Jesus offered.

But the Biblical narrative doesn't leave us in a state of despair. It offers hope, redemption, and a way out of the materialistic maze. Apostle Paul, once a man of status and influence, found this path. He wrote to the Philippians, *"But whatever gain I had, I counted as loss for the sake of Christ. Indeed, I count everything as loss because of the surpassing worth of knowing Christ Jesus my Lord"* (Philippians 3:7-8). The term "zēmia" in Greek, translated as "loss," suggests damage or detriment. Paul considered his prior gains, his status, and even his righteousness as a Pharisee, as detrimental when compared to the immeasurable value of knowing Christ.

This is the crux of the message for modern believers navigating their way through the trading floors of life. The allure of Tyre, with its gold and silver, is ever-present, but so is the opportunity to redefine our values, realign our hearts, and rediscover the treasure of a relationship with God. As Jesus stated, *"What good is it for someone to gain the whole world, yet forfeit their soul?"* (Mark 8:36).

The stories from Tyre's trading floors serve as mirrors, reflecting our own inclinations and potential pitfalls. They remind us to constantly evaluate where we are laying our treasures. While the city's ruins today stand as silent witnesses to its former glory, its lessons are as alive and relevant as ever. It's a call to introspection, a challenge to prioritize, and an invitation to trade the fleeting for the eternal.

CHAPTER 9

Floor Two – Jezebel

The very name "Jezebel" is synonymous with manipulation, control, and rebellion. This notorious queen from the Old Testament was not just a symbol of corruption; she embodied the spirit of seduction and cunning that continues to be a pervasive force in societies today. To fully appreciate the dangers she represents, it's crucial to delve into her history, understand her methods, and discern the spiritual implications of the influences she exerts.

Jezebel was the daughter of Ethbaal, the king of Tyre. Married to King Ahab of Israel, she brought with her the pagan practices and gods of her homeland, most notably the worship of Baal. This was not just a simple melding of cultural beliefs; it was a calculated attempt to undermine and eradicate the worship of Yahweh in Israel. The Bible tells us that Ahab *"did more to provoke the Lord, the God of Israel, to anger than all the kings of Israel who were before him"* (1 Kings 16:33). Much of this spiritual degradation can be traced back to Jezebel's influence.

At the heart of Jezebel's story is the Hebrew term "zānah," which can mean "to commit fornication" but can also be used metaphorically for idolatry. Through Jezebel's promotion of Baal worship, Israel was essentially "committing fornication" with other gods, forsaking their covenant relationship with Yahweh.

Her methods were neither subtle nor passive. Jezebel didn't just promote her gods; she sought to eliminate the prophets of Yahweh, leading a massacre that saw many of them killed. This political maneuvering was a clear display of the Greek concept of "kratos," meaning "dominance" or "rule." With an iron hand and a cunning mind, Jezebel ensured her beliefs dominated the spiritual landscape, pushing God's prophets into hiding.

However, Jezebel's manipulations were not just in the realm of religious practices. Her story with Naboth's vineyard provides a grim view of her political and emotional manipulations. Naboth, a man who simply desired to keep his ancestral inheritance, became a victim of Jezebel's schemes. When King Ahab expressed a desire for Naboth's vineyard and was met with refusal, Jezebel's reaction was swift and deadly. Using deceit and the machinery of state, she arranged for false witnesses to accuse Naboth of blasphemy, leading to his execution and the subsequent seizure of his vineyard (1 Kings 21).

It's in this narrative that we see the manifestation of the Hebrew concept "mirmāh," which translates to "deceit" or "guile." Jezebel's manipulations were not just aimed at fulfilling her husband's desires but were also a show of power, a declaration that no one could stand against her.

As we analyse Jezebel's life, we also find themes related to sexual manipulation. While the biblical accounts do not overtly describe her using her sexuality as a weapon, the archetype of Jezebel in popular culture and later Christian traditions often portrays her as the seductress, a woman who uses her allure to manipulate and control those around her. This interpretation can be linked to the broader themes of seduction that her character embodies – seduction not just in a physical sense but also in terms of leading people away from true worship and into idolatry.

Revelations 2:20-23 speaks of a spiritual "Jezebel," a prophetess who misleads God's servants into sexual immorality and eating food sacrificed to idols. Here, her name is symbolic, representing the culmination of all her manipulative attributes – emotional, political, and sexual. The Greek term "planaó" is employed here, meaning "to lead astray" or "to deceive." It is a stark warning against the seductive, misleading forces that seek to draw believers away from the path of righteousness.

The influence of Jezebel, both historical and symbolic, stands as a reminder of the multifaceted dangers believers face. The forces she represents – idolatry, political power plays, emotional manipulation, and sexual seduction – are not relics of the past. They're alive and active, seeking avenues to lead many astray.

In a world where power dynamics constantly shift and where seductive influences beckon at every turn, understanding Jezebel's narrative is more than just a historical exploration. It's a call to vigilance, a plea for discernment, and a reminder that the battle for our hearts and minds is unrelenting. To navigate this floor successfully, believers must gird themselves with the truth, stand firm in their convictions, and constantly guard against the subtle lures that seek to pull them away from their divine calling.

In understanding Jezebel's pervasive influence, one must also recognize the mechanisms she employed and the counterparts these tactics find in the contemporary world. There's an urgent need to illuminate her methods further, drawing parallels between the ancient and modern manifestations of manipulation, control, and rebellion.

The modern era, much like Jezebel's time, is fraught with voices that seek to divert attention and allegiance away from divine truth. Social media platforms, popular culture, and even political landscapes are imbued with varying degrees of manipulation, coercion, and seduction. In the midst of these influences, it becomes increasingly challenging to discern genuine voices from misleading ones. The Scripture warns, *"See to it that no one takes you captive by philosophy and empty deceit, according to human tradition, according to the elemental spirits of the world, and not according to Christ"* (Colossians 2:8). This warning feels more relevant today than ever.

Consider the pervasive nature of 'fake news' or disinformation campaigns. These can be seen as the modern-day equivalent of Jezebel's false witnesses against Naboth. Just as she planted deceitful testimonies to achieve her goals, the internet is rife with false narratives designed to manipulate public perception. This aligns with the Hebrew term "sheqer," which translates to "lie" or "falsehood." As believers, the challenge is to sift through the overwhelming information deluge, discerning truth from falsehood.

Furthermore, emotional manipulation, a tactic deeply ingrained in Jezebel's repertoire, is rampant in today's advertising and media industries. Advertisements frequently appeal to viewers' fears, insecurities, or desires, urging them towards a specific action or purchase. These tactics are eerily reminiscent of Jezebel's manner of playing on Ahab's emotions, capitalizing on his moment of vulnerability to propel her own agenda.

Political manipulation is another area where parallels can be drawn. While Jezebel used her position and power to enforce idolatry and suppress the worship of Yahweh, contemporary political landscapes occasionally witness leaders who, overtly or covertly, prioritize policies that undermine biblical principles. In such scenarios, it's crucial to understand the Greek term "exousia," which translates to "authority" or "power." While earthly authorities have their role, they are ultimately subordinate to divine authority. It serves as a reminder for believers to remain anchored in their faith and not be swayed by political currents that diverge from God's word.

Sexual manipulation, too, has evolved in its presentation but remains a potent tool in the modern arsenal of seduction. Contemporary culture, with its overt sexualization in entertainment, advertising, and even daily interactions, can lead believers down a path where physical desires overshadow spiritual pursuits. This resonates with the Pauline admonition in 1 Thessalonians 4:3-5, *"For this is the will of God, your sanctification: that you abstain from sexual immorality; that each one of you know how to control his own body in holiness and honor, not in the passion of lust like the Gentiles who do not know God."*

However, amidst these challenges, there's hope. Just as Elijah stood defiant against Jezebel's threats, modern believers are not powerless against the forces that seek to derail their spiritual journey. The Scriptures provide the necessary tools and wisdom to navigate these treacherous terrains.

Ephesians 6 speaks of the armor of God, a divine provision designed to shield believers from the multifarious attacks of the enemy. When Paul speaks of the "shield of faith," "helmet of salvation," and the "sword of the Spirit, which is the word of God," he is emphasizing the indispensable nature of these defenses in the face of deceit, manipulation, and seduction. These tools not only offer protection but also empower believers to challenge and counteract misleading influences, much like how Elijah confronted the prophets of Baal.

The story of Jezebel also serves as a cautionary tale of accountability. Despite her power and influence, she faced a tragic end. This can be seen as a manifestation of the biblical principle that *"God is not mocked; for whatever a man sows, this he will also reap"* (Galatians 6:7). It underscores the reality that earthly power and manipulation, no matter how potent, are transient and ultimately answerable to divine justice.

While Jezebel's story is rooted in ancient history, its implications resonate profoundly in today's world. Her tactics, though adapted to contemporary contexts, continue to challenge believers' faith and commitment. Yet, armed with the truth of the Scriptures, the guidance of the Holy Spirit, and the armour of God, believers can effectively confront, counter, and conquer these influences, ensuring their spiritual journey remains untainted and true to their divine calling.

CHAPTER 10

Floor Three – Athaliah

The tapestry of biblical history is replete with complex characters, among which Athaliah stands out as a paramount example of power, corruption, and spiritual derailment. The only reigning queen of Judah, her story offers a profound reflection on the perils of seeking power without integrity, the dangers of a poor self-image, and the profound implications of ties that bind beyond the obvious.

The legacy of Athaliah springs from her very lineage – the House of Ahab and Jezebel, a dynasty synonymous with idolatry and rebellion against Yahweh. But her influence wasn't limited to her own actions; it is also evident in the realm of self-image and identity. Her story mirrors many people today who grapple with self-worth, attempting to define themselves by external metrics rather than inherent divine value.

Scripture says, *"For you formed my inward parts; you knitted me together in my mother's womb. I praise you, for I am fearfully and wonderfully made"* (Psalm 139:13-14). Here, the psalmist captures the essence of our creation: we are intentionally and lovingly crafted by God. But Athaliah, influenced by her parental lineage, seemingly lost sight of this truth. Instead of grounding her identity in God's design, she anchored it in earthly power, leading her to trade her divine purpose for worldly ambition.

This quest for power made her enact one of the most heinous acts recorded in scripture: the massacre of her own royal family, aiming to consolidate her reign. *"When Athaliah the mother of Ahaziah saw that her son was dead, she arose and destroyed all the royal offspring"* (2 Kings 11:1). While this is a literal representation of her treachery, it is emblematic of a deeper spiritual malaise. Many, like Athaliah, sabotage their spiritual heritage, influenced by the lies they believe about themselves. The Hebrew term "sheqer," meaning deception or falsehood, aptly captures the essence of these misleading beliefs.

Another layer of Athaliah's influence revolves around the concept of masonic ties or alliances that are devoid of divine sanction. Masonic ties, in many theological discussions, refer to bonds or allegiances that are deeply rooted in mystery, secrecy, and, often, spiritual compromise. The term 'masonic' derives from the craft of stone masonry but has taken on deeper symbolic meanings over time. These ties can be interpreted as binding agreements that pull individuals away from their divine destiny.

Drawing a parallel to Athaliah's time, she formed unholy alliances, steering Judah into Baal worship through her rulership. *"He also walked in the ways of the house of Ahab, for his mother was his counselor in doing wickedly"* (2 Chronicles 22:3). This reference elucidates how Athaliah's counsel, stemming from her masonic ties to Baal worship and her family's idolatrous practices, led King Ahaziah and Judah astray.

The challenge that believers face in the modern age is not very different from that of ancient Judah. The contemporary world is rife with opportunities to forge alliances that might seem beneficial in the short run but can jeopardize one's spiritual journey in the long term. The Greek word "symbibazó," meaning to conjoin or unite closely, offers an insight. In the context of the New Testament, Paul uses it in Colossians 2:2, emphasizing the unity of love. But when such unity veers off from divine love and aligns with worldly or secretive interests, it becomes a potential stumbling block.

Reflecting on Athaliah's reign, the destruction she wrought wasn't solely because of her personal ambitions but also due to the lies she believed and the unholy alliances she fostered. Her narrative serves as a clarion call for all believers. It's a call to introspection, a reminder to evaluate the trades we make daily. Are we trading our divine inheritance for fleeting worldly gains? Are we, knowingly or unknowingly, entering into allegiances that dilute our faith?

Athaliah's story doesn't merely serve as a historical account of a queen's treachery. It's a spiritual mirror reflecting the dilemmas of modern faith. It underscores the importance of grounding one's identity in Christ, discerning truth from falsehood, and being vigilant about the alliances one forms. For in these areas, the battles of faith are often won or lost.

The narrative of Athaliah echoes beyond the annals of history and becomes a palpable reminder for every believer. It speaks to the insidious nature of compromise, the destructiveness of power unchecked by moral grounding, and the tragedy of a life driven by false narratives about one's worth. Athaliah's story extends an invitation to all: an invitation to delve deeper, to question, and to understand the subtle trades we might be making at the expense of our spiritual well-being.

When considering the depth of Athaliah's treachery, it's worth pondering where it all began. It wasn't merely her lust for power. The seeds of her actions were sown in the soil of identity confusion. This sentiment is encapsulated in the Hebrew word "Tohu," often translated as "formlessness" or "chaos," and is used in Genesis 1:2 to describe the earth's initial state. In a similar vein, a life detached from God's purpose can descend into a formless, chaotic existence. This is the kind of life Athaliah led — one devoid of the clear purpose and direction that God provides.

The repercussions of Athaliah's identity crisis were vast. She not only led herself astray but an entire nation. Judah, under her influence, spiraled into idolatry and moral decline. This ripple effect showcases how personal trades, when made by those in influential positions, can have societal implications. Our actions, especially those driven by a skewed self-image or a misguided understanding of our worth, can impact more than just our individual lives. They can shape families, communities, and entire nations.

This concept ties back to the biblical principle of stewardship. In Genesis, Adam and Eve were given the responsibility of tending to the garden and having dominion over the earth (Genesis 1:28). This stewardship wasn't just about physical care but spiritual responsibility. They were accountable for maintaining the spiritual atmosphere and sanctity of their domain. Likewise, every believer has a realm of influence, a domain to steward. Athaliah's story underscores the importance of ensuring that this stewardship aligns with God's design and purpose.

The Greek term "Oikonomia" offers a profound understanding of this concept. Often translated as "stewardship" or "administration," it implies the management of a household or an estate. Used by Apostle Paul in Ephesians 1:10, it alludes to the plan of God to bring everything under Christ's leadership. In essence, every believer is entrusted with the "Oikonomia" of the Gospel – to manage their lives and their sphere of influence in a manner that aligns with God's grand plan.

The unraveling of Athaliah's life was also precipitated by the unholy alliances she formed. These weren't mere political alliances for the sake of governance but spiritual ties that pulled an entire nation into the abyss of idolatry. When allegiances are formed without divine counsel, they tend to lead one away from God's intended path. These ties, reminiscent of masonic bonds, can be very subtle, often cloaked in the guise of convenience, advantage, or even necessity.

Delving into the New Testament, the Apostle Paul warns believers in Corinth about being unequally yoked with unbelievers (2 Corinthians 6:14). The Greek term "Heterozugeō," used here, paints a vivid picture. It literally means to be yoked differently and was a farming term. When two different animals, like an ox and a donkey, were yoked together, they couldn't plow effectively. Paul, drawing on this imagery, highlights the spiritual principle that when believers form alliances without discernment, it hampers their spiritual progress.

Athaliah's reign, steeped in treachery and idolatry, came to an end through divine intervention. Jehoiada the priest, recognizing the degradation of Judah, orchestrated a coup that led to her downfall. This culmination serves as a potent reminder that God's purposes will always prevail, regardless of how daunting the opposition might seem. As the scripture says, *"Many are the plans in a person's heart, but it is the Lord's purpose that prevails"* (Proverbs 19:21).

In closing, the life of Athaliah serves as both a cautionary tale and a beacon of hope. It is a caution against the pitfalls of power unhinged from divine purpose, the dangers of a misunderstood identity, and the perils of unholy alliances. Yet, it also shines forth hope – the hope that no matter how deep the descent, God's redemptive plan will always find a way to manifest. For every believer, the call is to tread with discernment, to constantly evaluate the trades they're making, and to ensure that their lives echo God's purpose and design.

CHAPTER 11

Floor Four – Cain

T he narrative of Cain and Abel stands as one of the most profound stories of sibling relationships in the Bible. However, beneath the surface of this familial conflict lies a maze of complex emotions and spiritual insights that can benefit anyone willing to delve deep. The trading floor of Cain embodies the dangerous pitfalls of unchecked anger, unfounded accusations, and a heart driven by selfish motives.

Right from the inception, Cain's offering was found lacking in God's eyes. *"And in the process of time, it came to pass that Cain brought an offering of the fruit of the ground to the Lord. Abel also brought of the firstborn of his flock and of their fat. And the Lord respected Abel and his offering, but He did not respect Cain and his offering. And Cain was very angry, and his countenance fell"* (Genesis 4:3-5).

This initial rejection was the catalyst that set in motion a series of tragic events. However, before progressing into Cain's subsequent actions, it's essential to unpack the spiritual insights from the aforementioned scripture. What made Abel's offering more acceptable to God?

It's a matter of the heart and priorities. Abel offered the firstborn of his flock, signifying that he was giving God his best, his first fruits, a term which is significant in Hebrew tradition. In contrast, Cain's offering was from the fruit of the ground, which in itself is not inherently inferior, but the scripture does not specify it as being the best of what he had. This distinction is emphasized by the Hebrew word "Re'shiyth" which means "first" or "beginning", representing primacy and priority. Abel's offering was a manifestation of his heart's position towards God - a heart that prioritized God above all else.

However, Cain's reaction to God's rejection reveals even deeper heart issues. The Bible notes that Cain became very angry. This anger, as the story progresses, isn't just a passing emotion; it becomes a dangerous entity that consumes him. The Hebrew term "Charah" which translates to "burn" is used to describe Cain's anger, suggesting an all-consuming rage.

God, in His mercy, offers Cain a warning and a choice: *"If you do well, will you not be accepted? And if you do not do well, sin lies at the door. And its desire is for you, but you should rule over it"* (Genesis 4:7). Here, sin is personified as a lurking entity, desiring to master Cain. The Hebrew term "Teshuqah", translated as "desire", carries the connotation of an overwhelming craving or longing. It's the same term used in Genesis 3:16, suggesting a desire to overpower or dominate. Yet, God reminds Cain that he has the agency to rule over this impending threat.

Unfortunately, Cain's subsequent actions show that he succumbs to this dangerous emotion. Consumed by jealousy and anger, he leads his brother to the field and commits the first recorded murder in biblical history. What follows is equally telling. When confronted by God about Abel's whereabouts, Cain responds with a now-infamous line, *"Am I my brother's keeper?"* (Genesis 4:9).

This response is dripping with defensiveness and accusation. It's not just a denial of his heinous act but an accusation towards God. The tone and manner suggest a heart that is not only drifting from God but is actively accusing Him. The Greek term "Kategoria" encapsulates this sentiment. Used in the New Testament, it means an accusation or charge, and Cain's interaction with God echoes this sentiment.

However, even in this dark moment, God's response is one of mercy and justice. While Cain is punished for his actions, God also places a mark on him to protect him from being killed. This mark, a symbol of divine protection despite human failure, showcases God's grace even in the direst of circumstances.

Cain's life, post-murder, is one marred by wandering and aimlessness. His disconnect from God is palpable, and his lineage reflects the ramifications of a life lived devoid of divine direction.

As one navigates through the trading floor of Cain, it's a journey of introspection and caution. It's a vivid reminder of the dangerous path unchecked emotions can lead one down. But more importantly, it's a call to recognize the Cains within us – the suppressed anger, the latent jealousies, and the subtle accusations. Confronting these internal struggles is the first step towards ensuring that we don't trade away God's best for fleeting emotions and selfish motives.

The story of Cain is not just a narrative of a man who lost his way, but it serves as a profound mirror to our souls. As we further delve into the depths of this trading floor, we witness reflections of our daily struggles, misguided intentions, and misplaced priorities.

When Cain asked God, *"Am I my brother's keeper?"*, he wasn't merely seeking an answer to a rhetorical question. Within this query, we can sense a deep-seated struggle, one that plagues humanity even today: the conflict between self-preservation and selfless love. In Hebrew, the term "Shamar" is used to describe the act of keeping or guarding. It implies a responsibility or duty. But Cain's defiant tone in posing the question shows a man who had abdicated this divine duty of brotherhood and love.

Contrast this with Jesus' teachings in the New Testament, where He instructs us to love our neighbors as ourselves. In the Greek, the word "Agape" is often used to describe this form of love – a selfless, sacrificial love that seeks the highest good of others. It's the very antithesis of the sentiment that Cain displayed. Where Cain's heart was consumed by envy and competition, Christ calls us to a love that celebrates and uplifts.

Yet, in our daily lives, how often do we resonate more with Cain than with the teachings of Jesus? How frequently do we prioritize our needs, desires, and ambitions over those of others? The marketplace of today's world thrives on competition and one-upmanship. It's a world where success is often measured by comparing oneself to peers and where the drive to get ahead can overshadow the call to lift others up. This is the very essence of the trading floor of Cain – a place where personal gains are prioritized over collective well-being.

Another profound lesson from Cain's life is the danger of not dealing with negative emotions promptly. After God rejected his offering, instead of introspection and seeking divine guidance, Cain allowed resentment to fester. This unchecked emotion became the breeding ground for more severe sins. It's reminiscent of the scripture in Ephesians 4:26-27 which advises, *"Do not let the sun go down while you are still angry, and do not give the devil a foothold."*

This scripture provides two significant insights. First, it acknowledges that anger in itself isn't sinful. It's a natural emotion. However, when left unchecked, it provides an opportunity, or as mentioned in Greek, a "Topos" (meaning place or opportunity) for the devil. This unchecked anger becomes a doorway for more malevolent forces to influence our actions, as seen vividly in Cain's life.

Then there's the theme of reconciliation. After committing the act, there's no indication that Cain sought reconciliation with God. Instead, he seemed more preoccupied with the consequences of his actions, focusing on his impending punishment. This stands in stark contrast with the story of King David, another biblical figure who, despite his egregious sins, sought God's face in repentance, as detailed in his heartfelt psalm of remorse, Psalm 51.

The Hebrew word "Teshuvah" encapsulates the essence of repentance. It translates to 'returning' and represents not just a feeling of remorse but a genuine return to God. The difference between Cain and David wasn't just in their sins, but in their post-sin responses. While Cain seemed resigned to his fate, David's heart yearned for a restored relationship with the divine.

This brings us to a crucial question: How do we navigate the trading floor of Cain in our lives? The answer lies in constant self-awareness and self-examination. It requires us to regularly check our motives, prioritize God's kingdom over personal gains, and cultivate a heart of "Agape" love. Furthermore, when we falter, as humans often do, it's imperative to choose the path of "Teshuvah" – a genuine return to God.

The story of Cain serves as a sobering reminder of the consequences of misguided priorities and unchecked emotions. It beckons us to tread cautiously in our daily trades, ensuring we don't compromise our divine calling for fleeting worldly gains. But more importantly, it serves as a testament to God's grace and mercy, reminding us that even in our darkest moments, God's protective hand remains, guiding us back to His eternal embrace.

CHAPTER 12

Floor Five – Delilah

The figure of Delilah, as depicted in the biblical account of Samson, is one that has fascinated theologians, scholars, and believers for centuries. In her, we see an embodiment of seduction, allure, and the danger of succumbing to our base desires. Delilah's narrative provides invaluable insights into the human heart's vulnerability and the treacherous terrain of unchecked passions.

Delilah, whose story unfolds in the Book of Judges, enters the narrative as the lover of Samson, the mighty Nazirite judge of Israel. The Philistines, enemies of Israel, see in her a means to overcome Samson, and she becomes instrumental in their plan to weaken and capture him. For a promise of silver, she persistently seeks the secret of his strength. With each attempt, Samson misleads her, only to finally succumb and reveal the true source of his power – his uncut hair, a symbol of his Nazirite vow to God.

At first glance, one may surmise that Delilah's power lay in her physical beauty. But a deeper understanding reveals that her true strength was in her ability to tap into the desires of Samson's heart. She understood his need for intimacy, his longing for connection, and his vulnerability.

In Greek, the term "Epithymia" describes a passionate longing or desire, which often extends beyond mere physical attraction, delving into emotional and psychological territories. It is this deep-seated 'epithymia' that Delilah manipulated.

But why did Samson, a man blessed with divine strength, fall prey to Delilah's charms? This is where the Hebrew concept of "Yetzer Hara", the evil inclination within every human, becomes crucial. According to Jewish thought, every person has two inclinations: "Yetzer Hatov" (good inclination) and "Yetzer Hara" (evil inclination). The latter isn't necessarily 'evil' in essence but represents our base desires and passions. It's the part of us that seeks pleasure, often without regard for moral considerations.

Samson's interactions with Delilah reveal a man ruled by his "Yetzer Hara". Despite being aware of Delilah's repeated betrayals, he returns to her, entrapped in a cycle of lust and desire. His physical strength was unparalleled, but his emotional and spiritual vulnerabilities were evident. Here, we witness the paradox of human nature – where one can be mighty in one aspect and utterly weak in another.

The tragic downfall of Samson post his confession to Delilah is not just an account of a hero's fall from grace, but it mirrors the dangers each of us faces when we let our guards down, allowing our desires to dictate our actions. James 1:14-15 captures this process succinctly: *"But each person is tempted when he is lured and enticed by his own desire. Then desire when it has conceived gives birth to sin, and sin when it is fully grown brings forth death."* The Greek word used here for 'lured' is "exelkomenos", painting the picture of a fish being drawn out by bait. Delilah was the bait that drew Samson out, leading to his eventual downfall.

Yet, the story of Samson and Delilah isn't just a cautionary tale about unchecked desires. It's also about redemption. Even in his weakened, blinded state, Samson's final act was one of divine strength and justice, as he demolished the Philistine temple, fulfilling his role as a judge of Israel. This act underscores a vital biblical principle: God's grace and ability to redeem, no matter how far one has fallen.

For contemporary readers, the trading floor of Delilah serves as a metaphor for the seductive allure of worldly desires that can entrap us. It's not always the overtly immoral acts but can be subtle allurements – the pursuit of fame, the craving for validation, the lure of materialism. Each time we prioritize these desires over God's purpose for our lives, we step onto this dangerous trading floor.

But how do we navigate this floor without falling? The answer lies in constant spiritual vigilance. By immersing ourselves in divine truths, seeking God's wisdom, and surrounding ourselves with godly counsel, we can guard against the Delilahs of our lives. The apostle Paul's advice in 1 Corinthians 6:18 to *"flee from sexual immorality"* can be broadened to all forms of seductive entrapments. Fleeing might seem like a passive or even cowardly act, but in spiritual warfare, it's a proactive strategy.

The narrative of Delilah reminds us of the ever-present dangers that lurk, seeking to entrap our souls. But it also points towards hope – that with God's grace, even when we falter, redemption is within reach. The journey on this trading floor is fraught with challenges, but with divine guidance, it's one that can lead to spiritual growth and enlightenment.

Delilah's manipulation of Samson isn't just a solitary incident in biblical history but serves as a mirror, reflecting deeper issues humanity grapples with. At the core of this narrative is the age-old battle between the spirit and the flesh. Galatians 5:17 states, *"For the flesh desires what is contrary to the Spirit, and the Spirit what is contrary to the flesh. They are in conflict with each other."* This scripture rings true as we delve deeper into the undercurrents of the Samson and Delilah narrative.

The power of seduction and the resultant spiritual blindness is evident throughout the Bible. Just as Delilah lured Samson, King David was entrapped by the sight of Bathsheba bathing. Solomon, in all his wisdom, was led astray by his foreign wives and their gods. The Greek word "apatao," meaning "to deceive" or "seduce," captures this essence. It describes a person being led away from safety or truth and into harm or error. Such seduction isn't always sexual; it's any enticement that draws us away from God's best for us.

To counteract the force of seduction, we must first recognize its source. James 3:15 gives us a tripartite classification of wisdom – *"Such 'wisdom' does not come down from heaven but is earthly, unspiritual, demonic."* This verse underscores that not all knowledge or insight we encounter is godly. The unspiritual wisdom, in Greek "psychikos," pertains to the soul or the natural human impulses. This is the wisdom that prioritizes self over the spirit and can easily be manipulated by external influences.

Delilah, in many ways, personifies this "psychikos" wisdom. Her actions weren't driven by overt demonic intentions but by a worldly, self-centered agenda. She was offered silver by the Philistine lords in exchange for discovering the secret of Samson's strength. In her dealings with Samson, we can infer that she was ruled more by her desires and ambitions than by any sense of righteousness or love. It's a stark reminder of how the allure of material gains or worldly achievements can often blind us to spiritual truths.

Hebrews 4:12 proclaims, *"For the word of God is alive and active. Sharper than any double-edged sword, it penetrates even to dividing soul and spirit, joints and marrow; it judges the thoughts and attitudes of the heart."* This scripture holds the key to discerning and combating the seductions we face. Immersing oneself in the Word of God allows for a sharpening of discernment, enabling us to distinguish between what's of the spirit and what's of the flesh.

However, being armed with the Word isn't enough. The application is crucial. The Hebrew word "Shema," often translated as "hear," encompasses a depth of meaning. It's not passive hearing but involves understanding, internalizing, and acting upon what is heard. This active hearing is what's needed when we confront our personal Delilahs.

Further, the biblical story isn't just about personal battles but communal ones as well. Delilah's actions affected not just Samson but the entire nation of Israel. It's a poignant reminder that our individual actions have broader implications. The community plays a vital role in supporting and holding each individual accountable. The New Testament church, as described in Acts, thrived on fellowship, breaking of bread, and shared prayer. This communal bond acts as a safety net, helping its members navigate and overcome personal temptations.

Reflecting on the Samson-Delilah narrative from a Christocentric lens provides an additional layer of understanding. Samson's strength, betrayal by Delilah, and eventual sacrifice can be seen as a foreshadowing of Christ's journey. Just as Samson was betrayed by someone he loved for silver, Christ was betrayed by Judas for thirty pieces of silver. And in their final moments, both Samson and Christ made profound sacrifices that brought salvation to their people.

But, where Samson's story serves as a cautionary tale, Christ's narrative offers redemption. Romans 5:8 reminds us, *"But God demonstrates his own love for us in this: While we were still sinners, Christ died for us."* While the consequences of yielding to our fleshly desires can be dire, God's grace and the redemptive power of Christ offer hope and restoration.

The trading floor of Delilah is intricate, filled with enticements that cater to our fleshly desires. However, as believers, we are not left unarmed. With the Word as our sword, the Holy Spirit as our guide, and a community of believers as our support system, we can navigate this floor with discernment and wisdom.

In conclusion, while the seductive allure of the world, symbolized by Delilah, is ever-present and powerful, the believer is equipped and empowered to overcome. Through steadfast immersion in God's Word, active participation in a community of faith, and a deep-seated reliance on the redemptive work of Christ, one can not only resist Delilah's enticements but also emerge stronger, with a refined understanding of God's purpose and calling.

CHAPTER 13

Floor Six – Leviathan

The Leviathan, as described in the biblical book of Job, is a formidable and elusive creature. More than just a physical entity, its enigmatic nature has long been symbolic of grander spiritual challenges faced by humanity. *"Can you pull in Leviathan with a fishhook or tie down its tongue with a rope?"* Job 41:1 inquires. This rhetorical question captures the essence of confronting Leviathan, which in contemporary terms, manifests in the deceptions we encounter, especially through gossip, lies, and the images we portray on digital platforms.

The Hebrew word for Leviathan, "Liv'yāṯān," often signifies a twisting or coiling. It suggests not only the physical attributes of this sea monster but also the intricate, convoluted nature of deceit. Deceit often coils around the truth, obscuring it and making it difficult to distinguish the genuine from the counterfeit.

The presence of gossip, which can be seen as a modern form of the Leviathan's twisting, is rampant, especially with the advent of social media. Proverbs 18:8 remarks, *"The words of a gossip are like choice morsels; they go down to the inmost parts."* This imagery of words being consumed like delicacies underscores the human propensity for scandalous or sensational news. But the caution here is evident; just as unhealthy food affects our physical bodies, consuming gossip affects our spiritual and emotional well-being.

When the Apostle James describes the dangers of the untamed tongue in James 3:5-8, he mentions, *"Likewise, the tongue is a small part of the body, but it makes great boasts. Consider what a great forest is set on fire by a small spark."* It's fascinating that while James wrote this in a time without digital media, his words are even more applicable today. A single tweet, post, or share can spark a wildfire of gossip, spreading misinformation rapidly.

Alongside gossip, outright lies or falsehoods have also found a breeding ground online. The Greek term "pseudos" refers to that which is false – a lie, deceit, or untruth. Ephesians 4:25 advises, *"Therefore each of you must put off falsehood and speak truthfully to your neighbor, for we are all members of one body."* In the era of 'fake news,' discerning the 'pseudos' becomes paramount. The onus is not just on the receiver to verify information but also on the sharer to ensure its authenticity.

The challenge of Leviathan in the digital age is further compounded by the images we curate on social platforms. Often, there's a discrepancy between who we portray ourselves to be online and who we are in reality. This is a manifestation of a double life, which, in Greek, is termed as "diploos" – double or two-fold. Matthew 6:24 warns, *"No one can serve two masters."* Living a double life, one for social validation online and another in the real world, is a precarious balancing act that strains our emotional and spiritual health.

The book of Psalms mentions the Leviathan, stating, *"You crushed the heads of Leviathan; you gave him as food for the creatures of the wilderness"*

(Psalm 74:14). This victory over Leviathan points towards the ultimate power of God. Even in our struggles with modern deceptions, God provides guidance and clarity. As Psalm 119:105 illuminates, *"Your word is a lamp to my feet and a light to my path."* In a world teeming with 'alternative facts' and curated realities, returning to the unchanging truth of God's Word offers stability and discernment.

Furthermore, the New Testament offers insights into living authentically, especially in a world where pretense is rampant. Paul's letters often highlight the importance of genuine love, unfeigned faith, and sincere intentions. *"Love must be sincere. Hate what is evil; cling to what is good,"* Romans 12:9 urges. Authenticity in our interactions, both online and offline, becomes a testimony of our faith and our commitment to truth.

Understanding and navigating the Leviathan's floor requires more than just personal vigilance. The community plays a pivotal role in this journey. The early Christian church, as described in Acts, thrived on mutual accountability, shared teachings, and communal prayer. By embedding ourselves within a faith community, we equip ourselves with a robust support system. This community can act as a sounding board, helping validate information, offer corrective advice, and most importantly, provide prayerful support.

While the Leviathan's deceptive coils may seem overwhelming, especially in our digital age, believers are not left unarmed. The Word of God offers illumination, the Holy Spirit provides discernment, and the community grants accountability. Through these, one can navigate the floor of Leviathan, discerning truth from falsehood and portraying an authentic image aligned with God's purpose.

In deepening our understanding of the Leviathan, we find that its presence in our lives isn't just an external force to combat; it is also a reflection of our inner struggles and tendencies. The Apostle Paul laments in Romans 7:15, *"I do not understand what I do. For what I want to do I do not do, but what I hate I do."* This struggle to reconcile one's actions with one's spiritual aspirations can be seen as the Leviathan's twisting and turning within our souls.

When we engage in gossip, share unverified information, or present an enhanced version of ourselves online, we often do so out of an internal desire to be recognized, accepted, or valued. The ancient Hebrews recognized this intrinsic human need. The term "kavod" in Hebrew, often translated as "glory" or "honor," also carries a sense of "weightiness" or "importance." Every human has an innate desire for 'kavod,' to be seen and acknowledged. This intrinsic need, however, can easily be preyed upon by the Leviathan's deceptive influences, leading us to seek validation in the wrong places.

The Apostle Peter, who himself struggled with seeking human approval, especially evident during his denial of Jesus, later writes with profound wisdom in 1 Peter 5:6-7, *"Humble yourselves, therefore, under the mighty hand of God so that at the proper time he may exalt you, casting all your anxieties on him, because he cares for you."* Peter's transformation from a man driven by fear of public opinion to a stalwart preacher of Christ's message is testament to the possibility of overcoming Leviathan's internal twistings.

In this age of digital connection, the concept of 'kavod' or seeking recognition is amplified. Social media platforms are designed around engagement metrics – likes, shares, comments, and followers. Each notification can act as a mini-validation, a small dose of 'kavod.' Yet, as Proverbs 27:20 states, *"Death and Destruction are never satisfied, and neither are human eyes."* Our insatiable appetite for validation, if not directed towards God, can lead us deeper into the coils of the Leviathan, becoming more entangled in the web of deceit and misrepresentation.

So, how do we redirect this innate desire for 'kavod' or recognition in a healthy, spiritual direction?

Jesus provides a paradigm-shifting perspective in the Sermon on the Mount. In Matthew 6:1-4, He says, *"Beware of practicing your righteousness before other people in order to be seen by them...But when you give to the needy, do not let your left hand know what your right hand is doing, so that your giving may be in secret. And your Father who sees in secret will reward you."* Jesus emphasizes the value of private, sincere actions over public displays. The recognition we so deeply crave, He posits, is best sought from our Heavenly Father, who sees the deepest recesses of our hearts.

This approach requires a transformative shift in our perspective. Instead of the immediate gratification provided by digital affirmations, we are called to seek a more profound, eternal validation. The Greek word "apecho," often translated as "to have" or "to hold," can also mean "to keep away from." It indicates a deliberate distancing or disentanglement. Applied to our context, 'apecho' can signify a conscious effort to disengage from the trappings of digital validation and instead anchor our identity in Christ.

This isn't a call to shun digital platforms entirely but rather to approach them with discernment. James 1:5 assures, *"If any of you lacks wisdom, let him ask God, who gives generously to all without reproach, and it will be given him."* Seeking God's wisdom in our online engagements ensures we use these platforms not as tools for personal aggrandizement but as channels of blessing, encouragement, and positive influence.

Furthermore, engaging in regular self-reflection can be instrumental. The Psalmist's prayer in Psalm 139:23-24 is pertinent, *"Search me, God, and know my heart; test me and know my anxious thoughts. See if there is any offensive way in me, and lead me in the way everlasting."* By regularly inviting God to examine our hearts and motives, we can identify and correct areas where we might be succumbing to Leviathan's influences.

As believers navigating the digital age, armed with the wisdom of ancient scriptures and guided by the Holy Spirit, we are not defenseless against the Leviathan's coils. By recognizing our innate desire for 'kavod' and redirecting it towards seeking God's approval, by practicing discernment in our online engagements, and by fostering a heart of self-reflection, we can counteract the twisting deceptions of the Leviathan and walk in authenticity and truth.

CHAPTER 14

Floor Seven – Apollyon

In the mosaic of biblical symbolism, Apollyon emerges as a figure of destruction in the New Testament. Revelations 9:11 introduces him as the angel from the abyss, whose name in Hebrew is Abaddon, while in Greek, it is Apollyon, both names meaning "destroyer". Yet, how does the spirit of Apollyon manifest today, especially in relation to the gospel?

To understand this, we must first look at the gospel in its unadulterated form. Romans 1:16 declares, *"For I am not ashamed of the gospel, because it is the power of God that brings salvation to everyone who believes: first to the Jew, then to the Gentile."* At its core, the gospel is a message of transformative power, meant to pierce hearts and alter lives.

But have we, in modern times, watered down this gospel of power?

The word "gospel" originates from the Old English term "godspel", which translates to "good news." In Greek, it is referred to as "euaggelion". The "eu-" prefix indicates "good", and "aggelion" stems from "angelma", meaning "tidings" or "message." So, the gospel is fundamentally the "good message" or "good news" of Christ's redemption.

However, as with any message, the way it's delivered affects its reception. There's a looming danger, an influence, perhaps of Apollyon, where the essence of the gospel might be diluted to make it more palatable to modern ears. In trying to make the gospel 'relevant', there's a risk of it losing its revolutionary edge.

Consider the teachings of Jesus, which were often radical, confrontational, and countercultural. He spoke of taking up one's cross (Mark 8:34), of hating one's own life (Luke 14:26), and selling all possessions (Matthew 19:21). Such teachings defy the comforts and pursuits of modern society. The raw gospel challenges the status quo, and therein lies its transformative power.

However, the spirit of Apollyon tempts believers to avoid the uncomfortable aspects of the gospel, to focus only on God's love, while downplaying His holiness and justice. It's a trend to highlight God's blessings while sidelining the call to repentance and sanctification. It's a shift from 'deny yourself' to 'please yourself', as long as one believes in Jesus. This diluted gospel, stripped of its convicting power, is no longer the full gospel.

This dilution might stem from an underlying fear or embarrassment. The Greek word "aischyne" translates to "shame" or "dishonor". It's a feeling that might overcome believers when faced with the challenge of presenting the unfiltered gospel in a skeptical world. This "aischyne", possibly influenced by Apollyon, can push believers to present a version of the gospel that's more 'acceptable', one that won't lead to persecution or ridicule.

Yet, the Apostle Paul's life serves as a testament to the power of embracing the gospel in its entirety. Despite imprisonments, beatings, and threats, he remained unwavering. He writes in 2 Timothy 1:8, "So *do not be ashamed of the testimony about our Lord or of me his prisoner. Rather, join with me in suffering for the gospel, by the power of God."*

It's crucial for believers to introspect: Have we traded the true gospel for a more comfortable version? Have we succumbed to the spirit of Apollyon, prioritizing societal approval over God's?

To counteract this, believers must return to the Word. Hebrews 4:12 reminds us, *"For the word of God is alive and active. Sharper than any double-edged sword, it penetrates even to dividing soul and spirit, joints and marrow; it judges the thoughts and attitudes of the heart."* Immersing oneself in scripture and seeking the Holy Spirit's guidance can revitalize one's understanding and appreciation of the gospel's transformative power.

In confronting the influence of Apollyon on this floor, believers are called to a renewal of commitment, to bravely uphold the gospel's true message and to resist the temptation to water it down. Only then can the church be the beacon of transformative power it was meant to be, undeterred by the destroyer's shadows.

Delving deeper into the influence of Apollyon, it becomes crucial to understand the subtleties of his work, particularly in the context of the gospel's presentation. While Apollyon's outright aim might be to destroy, his strategies are often more insidious. He dilutes, distracts, and deceives, pulling individuals away from the heart of the gospel.

One of Apollyon's most potent weapons is distraction. In today's age, where information is abundant and attention spans are dwindling, the genuine message of Christ can become overshadowed by a myriad of other 'messages'. 2 Timothy 4:3-4 warns, *"For the time will come when people will not put up with sound doctrine. Instead, to suit their own desires, they will gather around them a great number of teachers to say what their itching ears want to hear. They will turn their ears away from the truth and turn aside to myths."*

This turning away doesn't always manifest as a rejection of the gospel. More often, it's a subtle shift towards teachings that align more closely with societal norms and personal preferences. It's a cherry-picking of the scriptures that resonate while ignoring those that challenge or convict. And herein lies Apollyon's craftiness – rather than pushing an outright rejection of the gospel, he promotes a skewed version of it.

A look at the church of Corinth provides an illuminating example. The Corinthians were proud of their spiritual gifts and knowledge. Yet, they had allowed secular influences to creep into their fellowship. Sexual immorality was rampant, and factions had emerged. They prided themselves on their freedom in Christ but often misused this freedom. Paul, in his letters, attempted to redirect them to the purity of the gospel, away from the dilutions that Apollyon's influence had likely wrought.

There's also the challenge of the prosperity gospel, which promises material blessings as a divine right for all believers. While God indeed blesses and provides for His children, the notion that faith guarantees worldly success is a distortion. Such teachings divert the believer's focus from the cross and self-sacrifice to materialism and self-gain. This, too, can be traced back to Apollyon's strategy of offering a more 'palatable' gospel that aligns with worldly desires.

This aligns with the Greek concept of "kenodoxia", which means "empty glory" or "vain glory". Derived from "kenos" (empty) and "doxa" (glory), it represents the pursuit of accolades, approval, and earthly success over true spiritual growth. When the gospel becomes a tool for self-elevation rather than a call to humble servitude, the spirit of Apollyon rejoices.

Moreover, in the age of social media, the portrayal of one's faith can sometimes become more about personal branding than genuine testimony. The Hebrew term "shav" means "emptiness" or "vanity". It's reminiscent of the dangers of portraying a polished, problem-free Christian life online, potentially leading others to feel inadequate or believe that Christianity promises a life free of challenges.

The challenge before modern believers is multi-pronged: to recognize the diluted gospel, to resist the allure of distraction, and to remain grounded in Christ's authentic teachings. Ephesians 6:11 instructs, *"Put on the full armor of God, so that you can take your stand against the devil's schemes."* This armor includes truth, righteousness, peace, faith, salvation, and the Word of God.

But beyond just recognizing and resisting Apollyon's influence, believers are called to actively spread the unadulterated gospel. Jesus' parable of the sower in Matthew 13 highlights various responses to the gospel. While some seeds (the Word) fell on rocky ground or among thorns, representing those swayed by deceit and worldly cares, the seeds that fell on good soil produced a harvest manifold. This parable serves as a poignant reminder that despite the challenges, the true gospel will always find receptive hearts and yield fruit.

In conclusion, while the influence of Apollyon is undeniable and pervasive, it's not insurmountable. The history of Christianity is rife with instances where believers, armed with faith and the Holy Spirit, overcame deceit and distractions to uphold and spread the genuine gospel. As modern challenges arise, with Apollyon's shadows looming larger, the call to return to the gospel's roots becomes even more pressing. Only by doing so can the believer truly counteract the destroyer's schemes and stand firm in their faith.

CHAPTER 15

The Watchman's Duty

I n the annals of biblical history, the watchman has always occupied a crucial role. He stands on the city walls, scanning the horizon for signs of potential danger, alerting the city's inhabitants of impending threats. This image resonates deeply when we consider the spiritual dimension. Every believer, armed with knowledge and discernment, is called to be a watchman, ever vigilant to spiritual threats and poised to sound the alarm.

Ezekiel 33:6 paints a vivid picture: *"But if the watchman sees the sword coming and does not blow the trumpet to warn the people and the sword comes and takes someone's life, that person's life will be taken because of their sin, but I will hold the watchman accountable for their blood."* Such is the weighty responsibility placed upon the watchman. With knowledge comes accountability, and those who recognize spiritual dangers are duty-bound to act upon these truths.

But what does this mean for contemporary believers? It's not just about discerning spiritual threats but also about being vocal about them. Today's society, rife with distractions and competing ideologies, presents an ever-evolving array of challenges to the Christian faith. The watchman's role isn't merely to identify these challenges but to actively guide others away from them.

Let's explore the Hebrew term "shamar", which means to "watch", "guard", "keep", or "preserve". It encompasses more than passive observation; it implies an active role in safeguarding what's essential. In Genesis 2:15, Adam was instructed to "tend and keep (shamar)" the Garden of Eden. This was not just a call to cultivate but to protect. In a similar vein, believers are entrusted to guard their hearts, the teachings of the faith, and the community from influences that might lead them astray.

The New Testament, in its original Greek, offers more insights. The term "gregoreo" means "to be on the alert", "to watch", or "to stay awake". It's used repeatedly in the context of spiritual vigilance. In 1 Peter 5:8, believers are advised to *"Be sober-minded; be watchful (gregoreo). Your adversary the devil prowls around like a roaring lion, seeking someone to devour."* This is a call to constant vigilance, emphasizing the ever-present dangers from spiritual adversaries.

However, recognizing danger is only half of the watchman's duty. Communication is crucial. One cannot merely see a threat and remain silent. The watchman must sound the alarm, alerting others to the impending danger. This is not an easy task, particularly in a world increasingly intolerant of absolute truths and moral clarity. Speaking out might invite ridicule, isolation, or even persecution. Yet, as Jesus said in Matthew 10:27, *"What I tell you in the dark, speak in the daylight; what is whispered in your ear, proclaim from the roofs."*

Historically, numerous biblical figures embodied the watchman's ethos. The prophets, often at great personal risk, relayed God's messages to a frequently hostile audience. Nathan confronted King David over his sins, John the Baptist critiqued Herod's immorality, and Stephen, before his martyrdom, boldly recounted Israel's history of resisting the Holy Spirit.

Yet, the role of the watchman isn't reserved for prophets or those with significant public platforms. Every believer is called t o this duty. Whether it's guiding a friend away from a spiritually harmful path, challenging a teaching that dilutes the gospel, or standing up for biblical values in the public sphere, the opportunities to act as a watchman abound.

Furthermore, the duty extends beyond just pointing out dangers. It encompasses guiding others towards the truth, acting as a beacon for those lost in the morass of modern spiritual confusion. Paul, in Acts 20:28-31, reminded the Ephesian elders of their responsibility: "*Keep watch (gregoreo) over yourselves and all the flock of which the Holy Spirit has made you overseers. Be shepherds of the church of God... I know that after I leave, savage wolves will come in among you and will not spare the flock... So be on your guard (gregoreo)!*"

In these turbulent times, the watchman's duty is more relevant than ever. The spiritual landscape is replete with challenges that require discernment, courage, and an unwavering commitment to the truth. Equipped with knowledge, bolstered by faith, and fortified by the Holy Spirit, every believer can and must rise to fulfill their sacred duty as a spiritual watchman.

The watchman's duty is further magnified when we consider the interconnectedness of the modern world. The proliferation of information – and misinformation – means that now, more than ever, there's a need for discerning voices to rise above the din. With the advent of social media, 24/7 news cycles, and a globalized society, we find ourselves in a unique era where a spiritual watchman's call is not just local but has potential global implications.

This global platform also means that the watchman must be even more discerning. Just as the biblical watchman had to determine between a false alarm and a genuine threat, today's spiritual watchmen must sift through vast amounts of information to discern truth from falsehood. James 1:5 counsels, *"If any of you lacks wisdom, you should ask God, who gives generously to all without finding fault, and it will be given to you."* The pursuit of divine wisdom has never been more crucial. It's not merely about identifying obvious heresies; it's also about discerning the subtle shifts in societal values, cultural narratives, and intellectual discourses that might slowly lead people away from the heart of the Gospel.

Another layer to the watchman's duty in the modern context is understanding the psychological and emotional underpinnings of today's challenges. The Hebrew word "nephesh" often translated as "soul," encapsulates the entirety of human experience – emotions, will, and intellect. Today's spiritual threats often target the 'nephesh', capitalizing on fears, anxieties, desires, and aspirations. Recognizing this, the watchman must be adept not just in scriptural knowledge but in understanding human behavior and its drivers.

Consider the story of Nehemiah, who took on the monumental task of rebuilding the walls of Jerusalem. While his primary challenge was physical reconstruction, he also had to contend with the demoralization of his people, external ridicule, and internal strife. He served as both a literal and spiritual watchman, understanding that the wall's strength wasn't just in its bricks and mortar but in the heart and spirit of the people behind it. His leadership combined practicality with spirituality, action with prayer, and vision with compassion.

Similarly, today's watchman must strike a balance. It's not enough to simply point out the pitfalls; one must also provide a remedy, a way forward. This involves not just identifying threats but also offering hope, guidance, and a return to the foundational truths of the Gospel. Galatians 6:1 offers a blueprint: *"Brothers and sisters, if someone is caught in a sin, you who live by the Spirit should restore that person gently."* The watchman's duty is restorative, not just corrective.

Moreover, the watchman's role has a deeply communal dimension. It's not an isolated post; it's deeply embedded within the community. The watchman doesn't just stand on the city's walls; he is part of the city. His or her well-being is intrinsically linked to the well-being of the community. This relational aspect underscores the importance of trust, integrity, and authenticity. One cannot effectively warn of dangers if one is not trusted or respected by those one seeks to protect.

This leads us to an essential question: What fuels the watchman? Is it a sense of duty? A burden for the truth? While these are undoubtedly components, the core driving force is love. In Hebrew, the term "ahavah" captures the essence of godly love, a love that is selfless, enduring, and seeks the highest good for its object. Without "ahavah", the watchman's warnings might come across as judgmental, harsh, or self-righteous.

In 1 Corinthians 13, often referred to as the "Love Chapter", Paul provides a profound insight into the nature of this love. He states, *"If I have the gift of prophecy and can fathom all mysteries and all knowledge, and if I have a faith that can move mountains, but do not have love, I am nothing."* This underscores that even the most profound knowledge, discernment, or spiritual gifts are of no value without love.

Being a watchman, then, is not just about vigilance and alertness. It's about embodying the heart of the Gospel, which at its core is a message of love – God's unfathomable love for humanity. Every warning, every call to return to the path of righteousness, every gesture of guidance must be infused with this love.

As believers, the call to be watchmen is not optional. It's an integral part of the Christian walk. But it's also a journey. No one becomes a watchman overnight. It requires growth, learning, failures, and recoveries. It's a post that demands humility, for even the watchman can falter. But with God's grace, steadfast commitment, and an enduring love for God's people, the watchman stands – ever vigilant, ever watchful, ever loving. The duty beckons, the horizon stretches out, and the call to guard, guide, and grow resonates. The watchman's duty, in all its gravity and glory, continues.

CHAPTER 16

The Tough Path to Truth

There's an old saying, *"The truth will set you free, but first it will make you miserable."* For many, confronting the truth, particularly truths about ourselves, is a difficult path fraught with emotional landmines and challenging self-reflections. The Bible is replete with tales of individuals who wrestled with the consequences of their actions and the sometimes painful process of self-awareness.

In the ancient Hebrew texts, the word "teshuvah" is used to describe repentance. It means "return" and implies a journey back to a rightful or original place. But this returning isn't just a physical or external act; it's a deeply internal, personal process of reorienting one's heart, mind, and spirit. It requires facing hard truths about oneself and one's actions, but it also promises restoration and renewal.

Take, for example, the story of King David. As the shepherd boy who became Israel's greatest king, he is often heralded for his victories, his psalms, and his heart that sought after God. However, even David, the man after God's own heart, faltered. The tale of his illicit affair with Bathsheba and the subsequent murder of her husband Uriah is a dark spot on his illustrious reign (2 Samuel 11). When the prophet Nathan confronted him with his sin, David could have denied it, justified it, or even silenced Nathan. But instead, he faced the painful truth and responded with, *"I have sinned against the LORD"* (2 Samuel 12:13).

The Greek word "metanoia" is another term used in the New Testament to describe repentance. It implies a change of mind or a transformative change of heart. In essence, true repentance is not merely about feeling remorse or guilt but entails a genuine change in direction, a turning away from wrong and a turning towards right.

The apostle Peter provides another stark example. His denial of Jesus, despite his earlier bold claims of undying loyalty, remains one of the most heart-wrenching episodes in the New Testament. The gospels record that after his third denial, the cock crowed, and Peter remembered Jesus' words. *"And he went out and wept bitterly"* (Luke 22:62). That moment of realization, the weight of his betrayal pressing upon him, could have broken Peter. But it became a turning point. His subsequent repentance and restoration were so profound that he became a pillar of the early church, even penning two epistles that form part of the New Testament canon.

Facing our past requires courage. It's a confrontation with our own frailties, imperfections, and, often, our deeply entrenched patterns of behavior. The patriarch Jacob's night-long wrestling with the angel (or God himself) by the Jabbok river (Genesis 32:22-32) can be seen as a metaphor for this struggle. The Hebrew name "Jacob" means "supplanter" or "deceiver", and for much of his life, Jacob lived up to this name, deceiving his brother Esau and his father Isaac. But that night, he wrestled, and as dawn broke, he was given a new name, *"Israel", which means "struggles with God."* His limp, a result of the wrestling, served as a reminder of both the struggle and the transformation.

But what facilitates such confrontation? Often, it's the undeniable realization of the consequences of our actions. The Prodigal Son's decision to return to his father was instigated by the dire circumstances he found himself in - a far cry from the wealth and luxury he once knew (Luke 15:11-32). But it's also worth noting that the son's return wasn't just to escape his situation; he recognized his wrong, admitting, *"I have sinned against heaven and before you."*

In both the Hebrew and Greek definitions, the essence of repentance involves returning and changing. It's about realignment. But this process is neither easy nor instantaneous. It's a journey. For some, like the thief on the cross beside Jesus (Luke 23:39-43), it can be a last-minute realization. For others, like Paul, it's a dramatic shift (Acts 9:1-19). And for yet others, it's a slow, painstaking process of growth and realization.

The tough path to truth requires humility. Admitting wrong, especially in a world that often values appearance over authenticity, is counter-cultural. But it's also liberating. It frees one from the chains of past mistakes and opens the door to grace, restoration, and a deeper relationship with God. As 1 John 1:9 assures, *"If we confess our sins, He is faithful and just to forgive us our sins and to cleanse us from all unrighteousness."*

Confronting our truths, our past, and our mistakes is indeed a challenging journey. It asks us to lay bare our souls, to delve deep into our hearts, and to face the sometimes-unpleasant realities of our actions and choices. But it also offers a promise - the promise of redemption, of a fresh start, and of a love that covers a multitude of sins. It's a journey worth undertaking, for at its end lies not just truth, but transformation.

Taking the difficult road towards truth and repentance isn't a solitary endeavor. Throughout the scriptures, we find a God who is not distant or indifferent but one who actively pursues the lost, offering them hope and redemption. In our personal journey of confronting past misdeeds and seeking to make things right, we do not walk alone.

Consider the story of Hosea, an Old Testament prophet. At God's command, Hosea marries a woman named Gomer, who time and again is unfaithful to him. Yet, each time, Hosea is instructed to pursue her, to redeem her, to bring her back into his household. This poignant and deeply personal narrative serves as an allegory of God's relentless love for Israel, despite her repeated unfaithfulness. *"Therefore, behold, I will allure her, and bring her into the wilderness, and speak tenderly to her,"* declares the Lord in Hosea 2:14. It's a picture of God not as a wrathful judge, but as a spurned lover, earnestly desiring reconciliation.

The theme of God seeking the lost reverberates throughout the Bible. Jesus, during his ministry, narrated the parable of the lost sheep (Luke 15:3-7). In it, a shepherd leaves the ninety-nine sheep in his flock to search for just one that has gone astray. When he finally finds it, he rejoices. Jesus ends this parable with a profound statement: *"Just so, I tell you, there will be more joy in heaven over one sinner who repents than over ninety-nine righteous persons who need no repentance."* This story illuminates God's heart towards the lost and His desire for repentance.

Repentance, however, is more than just an emotional experience or a fleeting moment of guilt. In the original Greek, the term "metanoia" denotes a transformative change of heart. It's about genuine transformation. Zacchaeus, the tax collector, provides a vivid illustration of this (Luke 19:1-10). Known for his corrupt practices, an encounter with Jesus leads him to exclaim, *"Behold, Lord, the half of my goods I give to the poor. And if I have defrauded anyone of anything, I restore it fourfold."* Jesus' response to this declaration underscores the transformative power of genuine repentance: *"Today salvation has come to this house."*

Yet, one might wonder, if God is omniscient, knowing our flaws and imperfections, why does He yearn for our repentance? It's because genuine repentance leads to restored relationships. Sin, at its core, is relational. It creates a chasm between humanity and God, a rift that only repentance can heal. The prophet Isaiah encapsulates this when he writes, *"But your iniquities have separated you from your God; your sins have hidden his face from you, so that he will not hear"* (Isaiah 59:2).

Moreover, repentance has implications not just for our relationship with God but also with others. The tale of Joseph and his brothers in Genesis is a compelling testament to this. Joseph, after being sold into slavery by his jealous siblings, eventually rises to power in Egypt. Years later, when the land is hit by a severe famine, his brothers come to Egypt seeking food. Unaware of Joseph's identity, they find themselves at his mercy. It's a narrative replete with themes of deceit, betrayal, but ultimately, forgiveness and reconciliation. When the brothers eventually recognize the gravity of their misdeeds, Joseph's response is telling: *"Do not be distressed or angry with yourselves because you sold me here, for God sent me before you to preserve life"* (Genesis 45:5).

This narrative underscores the transformative potential of repentance and its power to mend broken relationships. It challenges us to confront not only our vertical relationship with God but also our horizontal relationships with those around us. As the Apostle Paul writes in 2 Corinthians 7:10, *"Godly sorrow brings repentance that leads to salvation and leaves no regret, but worldly sorrow brings death."* True repentance, rooted in a genuine realization of one's misdeeds and a desire to change, has the power to heal, restore, and rejuvenate.

In our journey towards confronting the truths of our past and the implications of our actions, we're not left to our devices. The scriptures paint a picture of a compassionate, loving God who not only desires our return but actively facilitates it. He is the shepherd searching for the lost sheep, the father eagerly awaiting the return of his prodigal son, and the kinsman-redeemer who seeks to restore that which was lost.

As we tread this challenging path, we're buoyed by the hope that, in our moments of deepest remorse and earnest seeking, we find a God who is ready to embrace, restore, and renew. The journey, though tough, is not taken in isolation. It's a collaborative endeavor, a dance between the divine and the human, ultimately leading to redemption and restoration.

CHAPTER 17

Into the Courts of Heaven

In the vast expanse of biblical literature, we encounter not just laws, commandments, and principles that guide earthly conduct, but also an intricate, divine judicial system that operates in the heavenly realms. The concept of the heavenly court system is not merely allegorical; it finds its roots in several passages in scripture, offering believers a framework to address spiritual matters with eternal implications.

The Book of Job provides one of the earliest glimpses into this celestial courtroom. Job 1:6 mentions, *"Now there was a day when the sons of God came to present themselves before the Lord, and Satan also came among them."* Here, we observe a formal gathering, a convocation of heavenly beings before the throne of God. Satan, the accuser, presents his case against Job, challenging his piety and asserting that his righteousness is merely a result of divine favor and protection.

Similarly, in Zechariah 3:1-5, the prophet Zechariah is shown a vision of Joshua the high priest standing before the Angel of the Lord, with Satan at his right hand to oppose him. Here, again, we observe the dynamics of the heavenly court. The Lord rebukes Satan, and Joshua, representing Israel, is granted a change of garments, symbolizing the nation's purification from sin.

These scriptures illuminate a profound truth: the spiritual battles we face are not solely waged on an earthly plane. There is a legal dimension in the heavens, and our actions, decisions, and especially our ungodly trades, have ramifications that echo in these celestial chambers.

The term "ungodly trades" might seem foreign to some, but in essence, it signifies choices where we exchange God's divine purpose and will for our lives for momentary gains or desires. These trades are spiritual contracts, and they have legal standing in the heavenly realms. So, how does one address these contracts? The answer lies in understanding and engaging with the courts of heaven.

The term "court" in Hebrew is "bet din." It refers to a place of judgment or a legal assembly. But the heavenly court is not just about judgment; it's a place of grace, mercy, and redemption. Hebrews 4:16 encourages us: *"Let us then approach God's throne of grace with confidence, so that we may receive mercy and find grace to help us in our time of need."* Our advocacy in this court is Christ Jesus. As 1 John 2:1 states, "...But if anybody does sin, we have an advocate with the Father—Jesus Christ, the Righteous One."

Understanding our position is crucial. In the heavenly court, we do not stand as the accused, defenseless and alone. Instead, we have Jesus, our intercessor, who has already paid the price for our sins and ungodly trades. He presents His blood as evidence of our redemption.

But participation in this court requires more than just awareness; it requires action. The believer must actively repent for the ungodly trades made, renounce them, and ask for their annulment in the heavenly court. This act isn't merely symbolic. It's a spiritual transaction, seeking to undo the spiritual contracts that might have been formed knowingly or unknowingly.

Daniel's prayer in Daniel 9 offers a blueprint. In this heartfelt plea, Daniel doesn't just seek forgiveness for his sins but also the sins of his people. He understands that Israel's exile isn't just a result of their actions but also the ungodly trades they've made over generations. In deep humility and repentance, Daniel petitions for God's mercy.

Engaging with the courts of heaven is not a one-time event but a continuous journey of aligning our lives with God's righteous decrees. It requires a discerning heart, one that is sensitive to the Holy Spirit's promptings. This discernment is crucial because not all ungodly trades are overt. Some are subtle, wrapped in good intentions and even religious activity.

In the Greek, the word "metakrités" means "an umpire" or "a referee." Colossians 3:15 says, *"Let the peace of Christ rule in your hearts..."* The term "rule" here can be likened to the decision of an umpire. Just as an umpire's decision in a game determines the course of action, the peace of Christ should be our "metakrités," helping us discern if we are in alignment with God's will or if we've entered into an ungodly trade.

As we delve deeper into understanding the intricacies of the heavenly court system, we realize that it's not about legalism but about relationship. It's about understanding our position and authority in Christ and ensuring that our lives, decisions, and trades align with the heart of God. In this continuous pursuit of righteousness, we not only find redemption for our past trades but also divine wisdom to navigate the future.

As believers venture deeper into the courts of heaven, they begin to comprehend the profound interconnectedness of their earthly actions with spiritual consequences. This revelation is not meant to instill fear but to provide a more profound awareness of the spiritual realm and our place within it. While our ultimate salvation rests on Christ's sacrifice, our daily choices can either amplify God's kingdom or diminish our spiritual authority.

One must consider Abraham, a figure central to Judeo-Christian beliefs. Hebrews 11:10 indicates that he was *"looking forward to the city with foundations, whose architect and builder is God."* This vision of a heavenly city didn't merely influence Abraham's perspective; it deeply affected his earthly decisions. For instance, when presented with a choice of land, Abraham allowed Lot to choose first, despite being the elder and having the prerogative to choose. Lot, driven by immediate material prospects, chose the fertile plains of Jordan, leaving Abraham with the less attractive land. Yet, it was Abraham who was later designated as the *'friend of God'* (James 2:23) and became the father of many nations. Abraham's interactions, decisions, and trades were rooted in a profound heavenly perspective.

When we dissect this further, we notice a trend in Scripture where the divine court is not only a place of judgment but also a place of intercession. Moses, after Israel's grievous sin of the golden calf, stands before God, not in a physical court but in a spiritual setting where the destiny of an entire nation hangs in the balance. He pleads for mercy, even offering himself as a sacrificial substitute (Exodus 32:32). Moses' profound act of intercession shifts the verdict from destruction to mercy.

The implications are immense. As believers recognize ungodly trades in their lives and the lives of others, they are not only called to personal repentance but also to intercede. Intercession, in the courts of heaven, is not merely about petitioning for needs but standing in the gap, presenting the case for mercy based on Christ's redemptive work.

The Greek term "enteuxis," often translated as "intercession" in the New Testament, carries the weight of a personal conversation or an interview. 1 Timothy 2:1 encourages believers to offer *"petitions, prayers, intercession (enteuxis), and thanksgiving..."* This signifies that our intercession is not just general prayers but personalized, specific, and intimate conversations with God about particular situations, people, or trades.

But how do believers ensure that their petitions align with God's will? Here, the Holy Spirit's role becomes paramount. Romans 8:26-27 mentions, *"In the same way, the Spirit helps us in our weakness. We do not know what we ought to pray for, but the Spirit himself intercedes for us through wordless groans. And he who searches our hearts knows the mind of the Spirit, because the Spirit intercedes for God's people in accordance with the will of God."* This Spirit-led intercession is the key to effective engagement in the heavenly courts.

Delving into Hebrew, the term "paga" can be translated as "to make intercession." It carries the idea of meeting, encountering, or even striking. In essence, intercession becomes the meeting point between humanity's frailty and God's sovereignty. As believers actively engage in this form of prayer, they can "strike" or "mark" situations in the heavenly realms, bringing about shifts and alignments in the spiritual atmosphere.

For those unfamiliar with these concepts, it may seem overwhelming. Yet, Jesus, our High Priest, set the precedent. Hebrews 7:25 states, *"Therefore he is able to save completely those who come to God through him, because he always lives to intercede for them."* Imagine the profound reality – Christ, seated at the right hand of the Father, is continuously interceding for believers. He is presenting His blood, His sacrifice, and making a case for humanity in the divine court.

The courts of heaven are not just a theological construct or a distant, intimidating institution. They are a reality, deeply interwoven into the fabric of believers' spiritual journey. As believers grow in understanding and actively participate in these courts, they unlock new dimensions of authority, intercession, and Kingdom impact. Engaging in the courts is not about highlighting one's spiritual prowess but about aligning with God's heart, bringing heaven's perspective to earth, and reversing the ungodly trades that have hindered personal and collective destinies.

CHAPTER 18

Practical Steps to Repentance

The beauty of the Christian faith lies in its promise of redemption and transformation. No matter the depth of our mistakes or the extent of our false trading, God's mercy remains endless, awaiting our genuine return. As it's said in Lamentations 3:22-23, *"The steadfast love of the LORD never ceases; his mercies never come to an end; they are new every morning; great is your faithfulness."*

But while God's grace is available, the path to truly accessing it and transforming our lives involves intentional steps of confession, repentance, and renunciation. These aren't just actions but deep, spiritual processes that renew our relationship with God and reposition us in the trajectory of our destiny.

1. CONFESSION: LAYING IT BARE BEFORE GOD

Confession, derived from the Greek word "homologeó," means to "say the same thing as another, i.e., to agree with, assent." When we confess our sins, we are agreeing with God about the nature of our wrongs. We're acknowledging our failures without justifying, minimizing, or deflecting them.

King David provides an insightful example. After his grave sin with Bathsheba and the subsequent murder of Uriah, he was confronted by Prophet Nathan. David's immediate response in 2 Samuel 12:13 was, *"I have sinned against the Lord."* He didn't attempt to rationalize but simply confessed.

For effective confession:

- Find a quiet space to reflect on your actions, thoughts, and motives. Psalm 139:23-24 can be your guide: *"Search me, God, and know my heart; test me and know my anxious thoughts. See if there is any offensive way in me, and lead me in the way everlasting."*
- Verbally acknowledge each sin. This isn't about feeling guilty but being honest.
- Understand the gravity. Recognize that sin is not just an act against a rule but an offense against a holy and loving God.

2. REPENTANCE: A HEARTFELT U-TURN

Repentance goes a step further than confession. The Greek word "metanoia" translates to "a change of mind," which in Hebrew thinking also implies a change of heart and action. It's not just about feeling remorse but about deciding to turn away from the sin.

The Prodigal Son's story in Luke 15 paints a vivid picture. He not only realized his mistakes but decided to return to his father, symbolizing a turn from his wayward path.

Steps to genuine repentance:

- Seek to understand the root of your actions. Why did you indulge in that particular sin? Was it out of hurt, fear, pride, or rebellion?

- Decide in your heart to turn away. It's not enough to feel bad; there has to be an internal resolution to change.
- Avoid environments or triggers that might cause you to fall back. If it's a relationship, consider distancing yourself. If it's a habit, seek alternatives or replacements.

3. RENUNCIATION: BREAKING THE TIES

Renunciation is the act of formally rejecting or disowning something. In the spiritual context, it involves breaking any ties or agreements we've made consciously or unconsciously with sin or demonic influences.

When the Ephesians came to faith in Acts 19:18-19, they not only confessed and repented but took an extra step: *"Many of those who believed now came and openly confessed what they had done. A number who had practiced sorcery brought their scrolls together and burned them publicly."*

For powerful renunciation:

- Identify any vows, promises, or spiritual agreements you've made. This could involve relationships, objects, or places.
- Verbally reject and renounce these ties. For instance, "In the name of Jesus, I renounce any ties I've made with [specific sin or influence]."
- Dispose of any objects or symbols that might have represented or facilitated the sin. This act, while symbolic, can be powerful in the spiritual realm.

Throughout this process, it's essential to lean heavily on the Holy Spirit for guidance and strength. Zechariah 4:6 reminds us, *"Not by might nor by power, but by my Spirit, says the Lord Almighty."* It's not about our strength but about surrendering to God's.

Furthermore, immersing ourselves in Scripture can be transformative. Hebrews 4:12 says, *"For the word of God is alive and active. Sharper than any double-edged sword, it penetrates even to dividing soul and spirit, joints and marrow; it judges the thoughts and attitudes of the heart."* By aligning our thoughts and actions with the Word, we progressively distance ourselves from false trading and draw nearer to the heart of God.

4. ACCOUNTABILITY: SHARING AND SEEKING COUNSEL

While our relationship with God is personal, Christianity is lived out within a community of believers. After recognizing our transgressions and taking steps towards confession, repentance, and renunciation, seeking out accountability helps reinforce our commitment to turn away from false trades.

Galatians 6:1-2 provides insight on this, *"Brothers and sisters, if someone is caught in a sin, you who live by the Spirit should restore that person gently. But watch yourselves, or you also may be tempted. Carry each other's burdens, and in this way, you will fulfill the law of Christ."*

For establishing accountability:

- Seek out trusted friends, mentors, or spiritual leaders. The wisdom found in Proverbs 27:17 states, *"As iron sharpens iron, so one person sharpens another."* Such relationships will serve as a source of encouragement and guidance.
- Be open and transparent about your struggles, allowing them to hold you accountable to the decisions you've made to change.
- Regularly meet or communicate with them. Their perspective and counsel, grounded in love, can be instrumental in keeping you on the right path.

5. REPLACEMENT: FILLING THE VOID WITH GODLY PURSUITS

When renouncing specific actions or mindsets, a void is often left behind. This emptiness can be a vulnerable spot, making us susceptible to revert to old habits or form new negative ones. Jesus illustrated this concept in Matthew 12:43-45 with the parable of the unclean spirit that returns to its former house, finding it swept clean, and then brings along seven other spirits more wicked than itself.

Steps to ensure a godly replacement:

- Engage in spiritual disciplines such as prayer, fasting, and studying the Word. These practices deepen our connection with God and strengthen our spiritual resilience.
- Seek out Godly activities that align with your interests. Whether it's joining a worship team, serving in outreach programs, or participating in Bible studies, filling your time with positive engagements reduces the likelihood of reverting.
- Continually renew your mind. Paul's exhortation in Romans 12:2 is pivotal: *"Do not conform to the pattern of this world but be transformed by the renewing of your mind. Then you will be able to test and approve what God's will is—his good, pleasing and perfect will."* This renewing is an ongoing process, fortifying us against old temptations.

6. RESTITUTION: MAKING THINGS RIGHT

Certain sins or false trades might have negatively impacted others, whether directly or indirectly. Part of the repentance process, when feasible, involves making restitution – aiming to restore or amend the damages done.

The transformation of Zacchaeus in Luke 19:8 is a striking example. Upon his encounter with Jesus, he declared, *"Look, Lord! Here and now I give half of my possessions to the poor, and if I have cheated anybody out of anything, I will pay back four times the amount."*

To approach restitution:

- Prayerfully consider those who might have been hurt by your actions or decisions. It's crucial to seek the Holy Spirit's guidance to avoid acting solely out of guilt or emotion.
- Determine appropriate ways to make amends. This could be through direct apologies, restoring stolen or borrowed items, or other meaningful gestures that show genuine remorse.
- Act swiftly but with sensitivity. While it's important to address the wrongs, timing and approach, especially in delicate matters, are crucial.

7. EMBRACE GOD'S FORGIVENESS AND GRACE

An essential aspect of this journey is truly internalizing God's forgiveness. Some individuals remain trapped in cycles of guilt and self-condemnation, even after undergoing the steps of repentance. This, in itself, is another form of false trade – believing that our actions are too egregious for God's grace.

However, 1 John 1:9 assures us, *"If we confess our sins, He is faithful and just to forgive us our sins and to cleanse us from all unrighteousness."* When we hold onto guilt, we inadvertently belittle the potency of Jesus' sacrifice on the cross.

In accepting God's forgiveness:

- Regularly meditate on Scriptures that affirm God's love and forgiveness.
- Declare these truths over your life, allowing them to reshape your self-perception.
- Celebrate your new identity in Christ, understanding that your past no longer defines you. As 2 Corinthians 5:17 states, *"Therefore, if anyone is in Christ, the new creation has come: The old has gone, the new is here!"*

The path to genuine repentance and transformation is multifaceted and deeply spiritual. It demands sincerity, humility, and a continual dependence on God's grace. But the fruits of such a journey – an intimate relationship with God, a clear conscience, and a transformed life – are beyond measure.

CHAPTER 19

Nurturing a Sensitive Conscience

Every believer embarks on an unceasing journey of spiritual maturation, learning to mirror Christ in character and actions. Yet, this transformational journey is often navigated through the compass of our conscience—a God-given internal monitor that discerns right from wrong. It stands as a sentinel, often nudging us when we verge into territories of negative trading. However, like any instrument, its efficiency hinges on its sensitivity, and the Christian life demands a particularly keen conscience.

The Apostle Paul speaks profoundly of the role conscience plays in his epistles. In Acts 24:16, he declares, *"So I strive always to keep my conscience clear before God and man."* The Greek word for "clear" in this context is "aponéō," suggesting a state without offense or, more vividly, being void of stumbling. Paul intimates the importance of a blameless conscience—one that's tuned finely to God's standards.

1. THE IMPORTANCE OF A SENSITIVE CONSCIENCE

Our conscience operates as a spiritual barometer, measuring our actions, thoughts, and motivations against God's standards. When misaligned trades loom, a sharpened conscience sounds the alarm. The Hebrew word "leb," often translated as "heart," captures the essence of this innermost part of us—where thoughts, will, and emotions reside. It's the seat of our moral consciousness.

Solomon, in Proverbs 4:23, admonishes, *"Above all else, guard your heart, for everything you do flows from it."* Guarding our 'leb' or heart requires vigilance, particularly in a world filled with distractions and diverging moral compasses.

2. DESENSITIZATION: THE GRADUAL HARDENING

While the conscience is a divine instrument, it isn't immune to external influences. Persistent exposure to sin, societal norms contrary to God's word, or even wrong teachings can sear it, reducing its effectiveness.

Paul warns Timothy of such a time in 1 Timothy 4:2, describing some who would come with *"hypocrisy of liars, whose consciences are seared as with a hot iron."* The Greek term "kaustériazó," translated as "seared," paints a graphic picture of branding. Like livestock branded by a hot iron, rendering the flesh underneath insensitive, so can our conscience become if consistently subjected to falsehood.

3. THE ROLE OF GOD'S WORD IN CALIBRATION

Hebrews 4:12 extols the virtues of God's Word: *"For the word of God is living and active, sharper than any two-edged sword, piercing to the division of soul and of spirit, of joints and of marrow, and discerning the thoughts and intentions of the heart.*" The Word isn't a mere collection of texts but a dynamic force, discerning our innermost motivations.

To nurture sensitivity:

- Immerse in God's Word regularly. Not merely reading, but meditative and reflective study, allowing its truths to permeate your heart and mind.
- Apply scriptural truths in real-life scenarios. James 1:22 cautions against being mere hearers, urging believers to be doers of the Word.
- Pray for the Holy Spirit's illumination when studying. The Spirit, the author of the scriptures, provides depth and personal revelations tailored to individual needs.

4. CONFESSION AND QUICK RECONCILIATION

One of the most potent tools for maintaining a sensitive conscience is the act of swift confession when we err. Every moment spent harboring guilt or justifying actions further dulls our spiritual sensitivity.

David, after his grievous sins of adultery and murder, cried out in Psalm 51:10, *"Create in me a clean heart, O God, and renew a right spirit within me."* The Hebrew term "barah" used for "create" evokes a sense of carving out, hinting at a heart deeply chiseled by God's standards. David's yearning wasn't for mere forgiveness but a complete heart overhaul.

5. FLEE FROM DUBIOUS SITUATIONS

While this might seem overtly simplistic, avoiding situations that might compromise our spiritual integrity is instrumental. Joseph serves as a poignant example. When faced with Potipar's wife's seductive advances, he didn't pause for reflection but chose to flee, as narrated in Genesis 39. His actions underscored a man attuned to God's standards, opting to preserve his relationship with God over momentary pleasure.

6. SEEK GODLY ASSOCIATION

The company we keep wields significant influence over our moral and spiritual compass. Paul, borrowing from Greek literature, admonished the Corinthians in 1 Corinthians 15:33: *"Do not be misled: 'Bad company corrupts good character.'"* Engaging with individuals who revere and uphold God's standards can serve as both a safeguard and a sharpening tool for our consciences.

7. CONTINUAL PRAYER FOR SENSITIVITY

The Christian journey isn't one embarked upon in isolation but in tandem with the Holy Spirit. Regularly soliciting the Spirit's aid in prayers, asking for heightened sensitivity and discernment, is invaluable.

Ezekiel 36:26 foretells God's promise for spiritual rejuvenation: *"I will give you a new heart and put a new spirit in you; I will remove from you your heart of stone and give you a heart of flesh."* A heart of flesh—a soft, pliable, sensitive heart, keenly responsive to God's nudges.

In cultivating a conscience finely attuned to God's standards, believers are better equipped to navigate the complex terrains of life, eschewing negative trades, and cleaving to paths of righteousness. The continuous pursuit of a sensitive conscience ensures a life that not only honors God but is also fruitful in every

8. THE ROLE OF TRIALS AND TESTING

Trials and temptations, contrary to popular belief, aren't meant to weaken the believer but to fortify their faith. James, in his epistle, commences with the exhortation, *"Count it all joy, my brothers, when you meet trials of various kinds, for you know that the testing of your faith produces steadfastness"* (James 1:2-3). This 'testing' in Greek is 'dokimion', which refers to the testing of the genuineness of something, akin to refining gold. Through trials, our conscience is sharpened as we learn to discern God's voice amidst chaos and choose His way over ours.

9. EMBRACING THE ROLE OF THE HOLY SPIRIT

The conscience, as essential as it is, still needs guidance, and who better to guide than the very Spirit of God? Jesus, speaking of the Holy Spirit, said in John 16:13, *"When the Spirit of truth comes, he will guide you into all the truth."* The Greek word for 'guide' here is 'hodegēsei', suggesting a leading or showing the way. The Holy Spirit serves as an internal guide, working in tandem with our conscience, pointing out areas in our lives requiring alignment, and steering us away from pitfalls.

10. THE PLACE OF GODLY COUNSEL

While the conscience is personal, there are moments we benefit from an external perspective. Proverbs 11:14 states, *"Where there is no guidance, a people falls, but in an abundance of counselors there is safety."* These counselors should ideally be those grounded in God's Word, providing insights and clarity when personal judgment seems clouded. Their external viewpoint can often highlight blind spots, helping realign the believer with God's standards.

11. REGULAR SPIRITUAL CHECK-UPS

Just as we undertake medical check-ups to ensure physical wellness, our spiritual health requires regular introspection. The Psalmist, in Psalm 139:23-24, offers a profound prayer: *"Search me, O God, and know my heart! Try me and know my thoughts! And see if there be any grievous way in me, and lead me in the way everlasting!"* This heart's cry is for a divine examination, a celestial audit if you will, to ensure alignment with God's paths.

12. EMBRACING REPROOF AND CORRECTION

Proverbs 3:11-12 advises, *"My son, do not despise the Lord's discipline or be weary of his reproof, for the Lord reproves him whom he loves, as a father the son in whom he delights."* Reproof and correction, though initially discomforting, play pivotal roles in refining our consciences. Instead of resisting or resenting them, embracing them ensures our spiritual senses remain attuned to divine frequencies.

13. GRAPPLING WITH GRAY AREAS

There are areas in life that aren't expressly addressed in the scriptures, leading to potential moral ambiguities. In such instances, Paul offers wisdom in Romans 14:23, *"But whoever has doubts is condemned if he eats, because the eating is not from faith. For whatever does not proceed from faith is sin."* The principle here is clear: if an action doesn't emanate from faith or conviction, it's advisable to refrain.

14. GUARDING AGAINST HYPER-SENSITIVITY

While a sharpened conscience is crucial, there's also a potential pitfall of becoming overly scrupulous, leading to legalism. Paul addressed this in Colossians 2:20-23, warning against human precepts and teachings that might appear wise but lack any spiritual value in curbing the flesh's desires. The balance is to be sensitive without being ensnared by human-made rules that don't resonate with the freedom Christ offers.

15. THE END GOAL: CHRISTLIKENESS

The overarching aim of nurturing a sensitive conscience isn't merely moral uprightness but a transformation into Christ's image. Paul, in Romans 8:29, elucidates this divine agenda, *"For those whom he foreknew he also predestined to be conformed to the image of his Son."* A sensitive conscience aids in this metamorphosis, ensuring every thought, action, and desire aligns with Christ's nature.

In a world replete with moral ambiguities, the believer's challenge is to navigate through, ensuring their actions not only conform to a moral code but resonate with God's heart. It's a journey of continuous refinement, of listening keenly to the soft whispers of the Spirit, and making course corrections as required.

By embracing God's Word, yielding to the Holy Spirit, and consistently evaluating our actions and motives, we can nurture a conscience that's not just sensitive but also aligned with God's purposes. It's a pathway not just of avoiding negative trades, but of engaging in those that accrue eternal dividends. In the grand tapestry of God's design, a sensitive conscience isn't an end in itself but a means to an even grander end: an intimate and unbroken fellowship with the Creator, reflecting His glory in every facet of our lives.

CHAPTER 20

Renewing the Mind

At the heart of spiritual transformation lies a profound, yet often overlooked truth: the battleground of our soul is primarily in the mind. Apostle Paul, with a sense of urgency and emphasis, beckons believers in Romans 12:2, *"Do not be conformed to this world, but be transformed by the renewal of your mind."* The word 'transformed' is translated from the Greek term 'metamorphoō', from which we derive the word 'metamorphosis'. Just as a caterpillar undergoes a radical change to emerge as a butterfly, believers are called to a spiritual metamorphosis, with the mind as the crucible.

1. THE MIND'S PRIMACY IN SPIRITUAL TRANSFORMATION

In the Hebraic understanding, the mind (often termed as 'lev' or heart in Hebrew) is more than just a seat of intellect; it encompasses will, emotions, and desires. Proverbs 4:23 admonishes, *"Keep your heart with all vigilance, for from it flow the springs of life."* This centrality implies that the quality of our spiritual life is tethered to the state of our minds.

2. THE DECEPTIVE ALLURE OF WORLDLY CONFORMITY

The world, with its plethora of voices and vices, constantly vies for our mental attention. Without even realizing, we can easily imbibe its values, paradigms, and perspectives. Paul warns in Colossians 2:8, *"See to it that no one takes you captive by philosophy and empty deceit, according to human tradition, according to the elemental spirits of the world, and not according to Christ."* To discern between Christ's truth and the world's deceit, our minds must be attuned to God's frequencies.

3. THE WORD AS THE AGENT OF RENEWAL

Psalm 119:105 eloquently declares, *"Your word is a lamp to my feet and a light to my path."* In the vast expanse of our mental landscape, God's Word serves as a guiding beacon, illuminating truths and dispelling shadows. Hebrews 4:12 further adds that the Word is *"living and active, sharper than any two-edged sword, piercing to the division of soul and spirit,"* able to discern the intentions and thoughts of the heart. Engaging deeply with the scriptures thus facilitates the process of mental renewal.

4. THE SPIRIT'S ROLE IN ILLUMINATION

While the Word provides the content for renewal, it's the Holy Spirit who catalyzes understanding and application. 1 Corinthians 2:12-13 says, *"Now we have received not the spirit of the world, but the Spirit who is from God, that we might understand the things freely given us by God."* The Spirit aids in internalizing divine truths, engraving them on the tablets of our hearts and minds.

5. SHATTERING STRONGHOLDS OF THE MIND

False beliefs, past hurts, and deceitful paradigms often fortify themselves as strongholds in our minds. 2 Corinthians 10:4-5 states, *"For the weapons of our warfare are not of the flesh but have divine power to destroy strongholds."* We destroy arguments and every lofty opinion raised against the knowledge of God, and take every thought captive to obey Christ." Through the dual agency of the Word and the Spirit, these mental bastions can be razed, paving the way for divine truths to take residence.

6. EMBRACING THE MIND OF CHRIST

One of the profound mysteries of the Christian faith is the possibility of possessing the mind of Christ. As Paul asserts in 1 Corinthians 2:16, *"For who has understood the mind of the Lord so as to instruct him? But we have the mind of Christ."* This doesn't imply omniscience but reflects a disposition that seeks to know and do God's will consistently.

7. THE CONTINUOUS NATURE OF RENEWAL

Renewing the mind isn't a one-off event but a perpetual journey. The verb form of 'metamorphoō' suggests an ongoing process. This requires daily immersion in the Word, consistent communion with the Spirit, and a vigilant guard against worldly influences.

8. THE OUTFLOW OF A RENEWED MIND

A mind anchored in Christ invariably affects every facet of life. Colossians 3:2 advises, *"Set your minds on things that are above, not on things that are on earth."* Such a heavenward orientation impacts our choices, relationships, ambitions, and overall life trajectory.

9. CONFRONTING AND OVERCOMING MENTAL LETHARGY

Just as the body requires exercise to remain agile, the mind too needs its regimen. A passive or lethargic approach to the scriptures can lead to spiritual atrophy. Delving into the original contexts, exploring Greek and Hebrew nuances, and seeking the Spirit's illumination ensures our minds remain spiritually agile and vibrant.

10. THE ULTIMATE VISION: REFLECTING JESUS

The ultimate vision behind renewing the mind is to reflect Jesus in thought, word, and deed. 2 Corinthians 3:18 encapsulates this beautifully, *"And we all, with unveiled face, beholding the glory of the Lord, are being transformed into the same image from one degree of glory to another."* Each phase of our mental renewal pushes us closer to this divine ideal, making us mirrors that reflect the very essence of Christ to a world in dire need of His light and life.

In this sacred journey of renewal, every believer is extended an invitation to partner with God. Through deliberate choices, consistent discipline, and an insatiable hunger for divine truths, we can transcend the base mould of this world, metamorphosing into radiant ambassadors of the Kingdom, bearing the very imprint of Christ in our minds and lives.

As we traverse deeper into the transformative process of renewing our minds, it becomes imperative to recognize the symbiotic relationship between knowledge and application. It's not merely enough to be 'hearers' of the Word; we must transition to being 'doers', allowing every revealed truth to shape our daily decisions and interactions.

The early disciples serve as apt exemplars in this regard. Their lives were not marked by passive absorption of Jesus' teachings. Instead, they engaged in robust dialogues, asking questions, seeking clarifications, and most importantly, implementing what they learned in tangible ways. Their encounters with Jesus weren't mere theological discourses; they were transformative experiences, reshaping their perceptions, priorities, and passions.

Consider Peter, a brash fisherman with a penchant for impulsive reactions. His journey with Jesus was replete with moments of profound revelations and equally profound mistakes. Yet, every encounter, every correction, and every affirmation he received was an opportunity for mind renewal. From his confession of Jesus as the Messiah to his subsequent rebuke for not discerning God's redemptive plan, Peter's mind was in a continuous flux, growing, evolving, and maturing. And by the time we encounter him in the epistles, we see a man deeply rooted in the knowledge of Christ, exhorting believers to a life of holiness, love, and perseverance.

But how do we, as modern-day disciples, navigate this transformative journey? First, we must foster a posture of humility. Recognizing that our current understanding is limited and always in need of refinement prevents the pitfalls of spiritual arrogance. The Greek word 'tapeinophrosýnē' captures this essence beautifully, urging believers towards a humble-mindedness that esteems others and acknowledges one's dependence on God's grace.

Secondly, immersing ourselves in scripture isn't merely an academic exercise; it's an intimate dialogue with the divine. Behind every verse, every parable, and every admonition lies the heart of a loving Father seeking communion with His children. This understanding transforms our approach to the Bible. No longer is it a manual to be dissected, but a love letter to be cherished.

Furthermore, as we internalize divine truths, it becomes imperative to translate them into action. James' epistle captures this succinctly, reminding believers that faith without works is dead. It's in the crucible of daily life, amidst challenges, temptations, and trials, that the efficacy of our renewed minds is tested. When faced with injustice, do we respond with the grace and righteousness exemplified by Christ? When confronted with personal failures, do we lean into God's mercies, allowing His truths to shape our self-perception? These are the litmus tests of a renewed mind.

Moreover, the journey of mind renewal is not an isolated endeavor. The early church thrived in communal settings, breaking bread together, sharing testimonies, and exhorting one another. They realized that collective wisdom, pooled from diverse experiences and understandings, enriched their collective pursuit of Christlikeness. In Hebrew, the term 'dabar' often used for 'word' or 'speak', carries connotations of purposeful, impactful speech. In the community of believers, our conversations, infused with scriptural truths, can serve as instruments of mutual edification, reinforcing the process of mind renewal.

However, this transformative journey is not devoid of challenges. The adversary, ever watchful, seeks to sow seeds of doubt, discord, and distraction. Misinterpretations, misapplications, and even moments of spiritual myopia are all possible. Yet, even in these moments, there's profound hope. Our guide in this journey, the Holy Spirit, is adept at course correction, gently nudging us back to the path of truth. The Hebrew term 'Ruach', often used for the Spirit, encompasses breath, life force, and divine influence. This Ruach not only illumines our understanding but breathes life into our efforts, ensuring that our quest for a renewed mind, though fraught with challenges, is anchored in divine enablement.

In this sanctified endeavor, moments of epiphany are interspersed with phases of seeming stagnation. Yet, every step, every revelation, and every act of obedience etches the image of Christ deeper into our psyche. Paul's prayer for the Ephesian church encapsulates this journey beautifully: that they may be strengthened in their inner being, have Christ dwell in their hearts through faith, and be rooted and grounded in love. This is the quintessence of mind renewal – a heart where Christ resides, a foundation rooted in love, and a life reflective of Kingdom values.

The invitation to this transformative journey is both a privilege and a responsibility. A privilege because the Creator of the cosmos invites us into an intimate, transformative relationship with Him. A responsibility because, as recipients of this divine truth, we are entrusted with the mandate to be salt and light, influencing the world with the flavor and luminance of Kingdom principles.

In the words of Jesus, as recorded in the Gospel of John, *"If you abide in my word, you are truly my disciples, and you will know the truth, and the truth will set you free."* Herein lies the promise and potential of a renewed mind: a life of authentic discipleship, profound revelation, and unparalleled freedom.

CHAPTER 21

Courtroom Prayer Explained

The scriptures are replete with legal language and courtroom imagery that provide a vivid picture of the judicial system of heaven. When used appropriately, these metaphors serve as potent tools to understand our position in Christ and the legal rights we possess in the spirit realm. One of the most intriguing and empowering concepts that emerge from this legal framework is the idea of "courtroom prayer."

The foundation of courtroom prayer can be traced back to Isaiah 43:26, where God says, *"Put me in remembrance; let us contend together; state your case, that you may be proved right."* Here, God invites His people into a divine courtroom, challenging them to present their case before Him. This isn't a confrontation, but rather an invitation to dialogue, where God, the righteous judge, is willing to hear our petitions and arguments.

The courtroom of heaven is not a space of intimidation, but of vindication. It is where the believer, armed with the truths of scripture, can present their petitions and see justice meted out. The Hebrew word "Riv" often translates to "contend" or "plead a case." It carries the weight of presenting an argument, of advocating, and of seeking justice.

Now, juxtapose this with the New Testament, where Jesus' parable in Luke 18:1-8 brings forth the narrative of the persistent widow. This widow, devoid of social standing or influence, approaches an unjust judge with her plea for justice against her adversary. Her persistence wears down the judge, and he grants her request. Jesus uses this parable to underscore the importance of persistent prayer and the faith that God will bring justice swiftly.

Yet, the courtroom prayer is not just about presenting petitions; it is also about confronting our trades – those areas of our lives where we've made agreements, consciously or unconsciously, with ungodly beliefs, patterns, or spirits. In these spiritual transactions, we may have traded God's truth for a lie or His peace for momentary pleasure. The courtroom becomes a space where these trades are exposed, dealt with, and where we can realign with God's original intention for our lives.

James 4:7 says, *"Submit yourselves therefore to God. Resist the devil, and he will flee from you."* This scripture captures the essence of confronting our trades in the divine courtroom. Submission is the act of presenting ourselves before God, acknowledging His lordship and our dependence on His grace. Resistance is the act of confronting the adversary, presenting the evidence of our covenant rights in Christ, and demanding a cessation of illegal activities in our lives.

The Greek term "hupotasso," translated as "submit," conveys the idea of aligning under, of ordering oneself under a specific authority. It's a military term, speaking of soldiers aligning under their commanding officer. This submission is not out of compulsion but out of a realization of the authority and protection that come from this alignment.

Furthermore, the courtroom prayer's efficacy is heightened when we understand our position in Christ. Ephesians 2:6 tells us that God *"raised us up with him and seated us with him in the heavenly places in Christ Jesus."* Our position is not one of a defendant, but of a co-heir with Christ, seated in a place of authority, advocating for justice from a standpoint of victory.

However, it's crucial to recognize that our role in the courtroom isn't to convince a reluctant God. Rather, it is to agree with what He has already decreed. In Greek, the term "homologeo," often translated as "confess" in the New Testament, means to "say the same as." Our declarations, confessions, and petitions in the courtroom are merely echoing God's word back to Him, aligning our hearts with His will.

Yet, courtroom prayer goes beyond individual trades. As intercessors, we have the privilege of standing in the gap, presenting cases on behalf of others, regions, or even nations. Abraham's intercession for Sodom in Genesis 18 is a vivid example. In a dialogue resembling a courtroom argument, Abraham petitions God, negotiating on behalf of the city. Though the city's fate was sealed due to its wickedness, Abraham's intercession bore fruit in the form of Lot's deliverance.

Understanding the dynamics of the heavenly courtroom and its implications empowers believers to confront and rectify their trades. It reminds us of our identity, our covenant rights, and the power of persistent, faith-filled prayer. The courtroom of heaven is open, and the Righteous Judge invites us to present our cases, assured of His justice, mercy, and unfailing love.

Delving deeper into the biblical landscape, we can glean further insight into the power of courtroom prayers by examining the lives and experiences of various biblical figures. These individuals, directly or indirectly, approached the throne of God, contended with Him, and in the process unveiled significant truths about the nature of God and our relationship with Him.

1. JOB'S PLEA FOR A MEDIATOR:

Job, amidst unparalleled suffering, wrestles with the apparent silence of God. In Job 9:33-34, he laments, *"If only there were someone to mediate between us, someone to bring us together,* someone to remove God's rod from me, so that his terror would frighten me no more."* Here, Job longs for a mediator, someone who could stand between him and God, advocating on his behalf. This plea foreshadows the redemptive work of Jesus Christ, our great High Priest and Mediator, who now intercedes for us (Hebrews 7:25). It's through Christ that our prayers, including those presented in the divine courtroom, find their efficacy.

2. MOSES - INTERCESSOR FOR ISRAEL:

When Israel constructed and worshiped the golden calf at Sinai, God's wrath was kindled. He contemplated wiping out the nation. Yet, Moses, in a profound act of intercession, steps into the gap. Exodus 32:11-13 records his plea, *"Why should your anger burn against your people, whom you brought out of Egypt with great power and a mighty hand? ... Remember your servants Abraham, Isaac, and Israel."* Moses essentially presents a 'case' before God, reminding Him of His promises. The result? God relented from the disaster He had considered.

3. HANNAH'S HEARTFELT PETITION:

The story of Hannah offers profound insights into how the earnest petitions of a broken heart ascend to God's throne. Desperate for a child, Hannah doesn't just pray; she lays bare her soul, pouring out her anguish and sorrow. Her prayers were so fervent that Eli, the priest, mistook her for being drunk (1 Samuel 1:12-16). But Hannah was presenting her case, her plea for a son, before the Judge of all the earth. In response to her genuine plea, God remembered Hannah, granting her Samuel, who became one of Israel's greatest prophets.

4. HEZEKIAH'S PLEA FOR LIFE:

When faced with a terminal illness, King Hezekiah turns his face to the wall and prays earnestly to God, reminding Him of his faithfulness and dedication (2 Kings 20:2-3). Hezekiah is not merely making a request; he's presenting a case before God, offering evidence of his wholehearted service. God's response? He extends Hezekiah's life by fifteen years. This account emphasizes that God hears, He sees, and He responds when we approach Him with sincere hearts.

5. DANIEL'S INTERCESSION FOR ISRAEL:

In Daniel 9, we find Daniel engaging in profound intercession for the sins of Israel. Recognizing the time of exile was coming to an end, he doesn't just pray for deliverance; he confesses the sins of the nation, aligning his heart with God's purposes. Daniel's prayer resembles a legal plea, presenting the historical faithfulness of God juxtaposed with Israel's rebellion. The angel Gabriel's swift response to provide understanding about the future of Israel underlines the effectiveness of such aligned intercession.

Each of these biblical figures, in their unique circumstances, ventured into the 'courtroom' of heaven, presenting their cases, not based on their righteousness but grounded in God's character and promises. Their experiences underscore the truth that God is not a distant, impersonal judge but a loving Father, eager to engage with His children.

The diversity of these prayers—ranging from personal requests to intercession for nations—demonstrates the expansive scope of the divine courtroom. It's a place where personal pains like Hannah's barrenness find solace, and national sins, like Israel's rebellion, find mercy.

Drawing from these examples, modern believers can be encouraged to approach God's throne with confidence (Hebrews 4:16). Our prayers, when grounded in God's word and character, have the potential to shift circumstances, influence nations, and above all, draw us closer to the heart of God.

By immersing ourselves in these accounts, we not only gain strategies for prayer but also encounter a God who passionately loves and relentlessly pursues His people. The courtroom of heaven, thus, is not merely a place of legal transactions; it's a space of divine communion, where God's justice and mercy converge, drawing us into deeper realms of His love and purpose.

CHAPTER 22

Personal Reflections and Testimonies

S tories of transformation echo through the annals of scripture, reminiscent of the deep and personal work God accomplishes in the hearts of individuals. The Bible isn't merely a historical account; it's a living testament of real people who encountered the living God and were never the same again.

Take, for instance, David, the shepherd boy turned king. In the quiet pastures, he penned songs of love and trust towards God. Yet, in the palace's confines, he fell into grievous sin with Bathsheba, and the weight of this sin led him to further wrongdoing. When confronted by the prophet Nathan, David's heart broke in contrition. He turned to the Lord, pleading in Psalm 51:10, *"Create in me a clean heart, O God, and renew a right spirit within me."* David's journey from sin to repentance, from despair to hope, provides a poignant testimony of God's ability to transform even a heart that has gone astray.

There's also the narrative of Rahab, a Canaanite harlot. Living on Jericho's walls, her life was marked by societal disdain and personal regret. Yet, upon hearing of the God of Israel, her heart was stirred with faith. She chose to shelter the Israelite spies, banking not on her deeds, but on God's mercy. Rahab's declaration, *"for the LORD your God, He is God in the heavens above and on the earth beneath"* (Joshua 2:11), signaled her transformation from a life of degradation to one of faith and purpose.

Fast-forwarding to the New Testament, the account of Zacchaeus offers a riveting testimony. As a tax collector, he was affluent, yet his wealth came at the cost of integrity and community respect. However, a single encounter with Jesus led to a profound transformation. He not only repented but sought to make restitution, declaring, *"Behold, Lord, half of my possessions I will give to the poor, and if I have defrauded anyone of anything, I will give back four times as much"* (Luke 19:8). Zacchaeus' turnaround is a testament to the transformative power inherent in a genuine encounter with Christ.

Mary Magdalene's life provides another beautiful canvas of redemption. Once tormented by seven demons, her life was a whirlwind of chaos and despair. Yet, when she met Jesus, she found deliverance and purpose. Her devotion to Him was so profound that she became one of the first to witness the risen Lord. Her testimony resonates with the words of Psalm 34:4, *"I sought the LORD, and He answered me, and delivered me from all my fears."*

But what does all this mean for contemporary believers? Can modern individuals experience this depth of transformation? The answer resounds in the myriad testimonies of believers today who have walked the path of recognizing their ungodly trades and have found wholeness in Christ.

Consider Sophia, a successful corporate lawyer, who seemingly had everything. Yet, beneath the surface, she grappled with the void of purposelessness. Her relentless pursuit of success was, in essence, a trade-off for genuine peace and joy. Upon hearing about the idea of trading in the heavenly court, she embarked on a journey of deep introspection. In her words, "I realized I had been trading God's peace for fleeting accolades." Through intentional prayer and genuine repentance, Sophia began to reorder her priorities, seeking first the Kingdom of God, as advised in Matthew 6:33. Today, while she still excels in her profession, her primary identity is as a beloved child of God.

Similarly, Michael, once ensnared in addiction, discovered that at the root of his bondage was a trade he had made — seeking solace in substances over the comfort of the Holy Spirit. He narrates, "I had traded the *Parakletos* (a Greek term meaning 'Helper', referring to the Holy Spirit) for a fleeting pleasure." By recognizing this trade and engaging in sincere repentance, Michael found freedom. Today, he mentors young men, guiding them away from the pitfalls he once fell into.

These testimonies, old and new, collectively proclaim the transformative power of God. They serve as beacons of hope, affirming that no matter how deep the pit, God's hand can reach in, pull us out, and set our feet upon the rock. From the pages of scripture to the lived experiences of believers today, the journey from brokenness to wholeness, from trading falsely to living authentically, is a testament to the enduring, redemptive love of God.

In the tapestry of redemption, every thread tells a story. Each individual thread, while unique, intertwines with others, creating a beautiful picture of God's grace and mercy. As we dive deeper into these personal reflections and testimonies, we recognize the universality of human struggles and the unparalleled depth of divine intervention.

Consider Esther, a young woman trapped in a cycle of abusive relationships. Each relationship, she believed, would be her ticket out of loneliness, only to plunge her deeper into a quagmire of pain. "I kept trading my worth, my *tzelm* (a Hebrew term for 'image,' signifying our creation in the image of God) for a semblance of love," she confessed. Esther's wake-up call came when a friend introduced her to the biblical story of Hosea, a prophet who marries an unfaithful woman, symbolizing God's unfailing love for His wayward people. The unconditional love displayed by Hosea mirrored the love of God, a love that Esther had been yearning for. Through prayer, counseling, and surrounding herself with a supportive faith community, Esther began the arduous journey of healing. Today, she runs support groups for women with similar experiences, offering them a safe space to encounter the boundless love of God.

Then there's Elias, a brilliant young academic who prided himself on his intellectual accomplishments. His accolades were many, and with every achievement, his ego swelled. But in the quiet moments of introspection, Elias felt a nagging emptiness. He had unknowingly traded the wisdom of God for human knowledge. The Apostle Paul's letter to the Corinthians rang true for him: *"For the wisdom of this world is foolishness in God's sight"* (1 Corinthians 3:19). Elias's journey to transformation began with a humble recognition of the futility of human wisdom in the face of divine truth. Surrendering his pride, Elias embarked on a quest for true wisdom, the kind that James describes as *"first pure, then peaceable, gentle, open to reason, full of mercy and good fruits, impartial and sincere"* (James 3:17). Today, Elias uses his academic platform not to elevate himself, but to point others to the inexhaustible riches of God's wisdom.

In another corner of the world, Naomi wrestled with the specter of her past. Raised in a household where occult practices were commonplace, she grew up with a distorted view of spirituality. These early experiences traded genuine spiritual encounters for deceptive ones. But during a mission trip, she met believers who introduced her to the power of Jesus' name. Drawing from the scriptures, especially passages like Colossians 2:15 where Paul describes how Jesus *"disarmed the rulers and authorities and put them to open shame, by triumphing over them in him,"* Naomi realized the authority she had in Christ. Over time, with prayer and deliverance, she broke free from the chains of her past. Today, she helps others find freedom from similar bondages, leading them to the true spiritual heritage they have in Christ.

Or the poignant tale of Samuel, who grew up in the church but traded genuine faith for ritualistic religiosity. His life was a checklist of dos and don'ts, devoid of a personal relationship with God. The parable of the prodigal son in Luke 15 became a mirror for Samuel. Like the elder son, he had been close to the Father in proximity but far in heart. The realization that God desired mercy and not sacrifice, relationship over ritual, led Samuel on a journey back to the heart of the Father. Today, he mentors young believers, guiding them in cultivating a vibrant, personal relationship with God.

Each of these stories stands as a testament to the transformative power of recognizing our trades and returning to the heart of God. The patterns are eerily similar – a trade is made, often unconsciously, leading to a void. But when that trade is recognized, and the journey of repentance embarked upon, transformation follows.

What's remarkable about these testimonies is the ripple effect they create. Esther's healing becomes a beacon of hope for many women. Elias's intellectual pursuits now lead many to the heart of divine wisdom. Naomi's freedom becomes a key to unlock the chains for others. Samuel's return to genuine faith guides many more back to the heart of the Father.

These narratives underscore a fundamental truth: our personal journeys of transformation are not just for us. They serve a greater purpose, pointing others to the redemptive work of God. They are, as Paul states in 2 Corinthians 3:3, *"letters from Christ delivered by us, written not with ink but with the Spirit of the living God, not on tablets of stone but on tablets of human hearts."* Through these stories, others can read and witness the transformative power of God, drawing inspiration and hope for their own journeys.

CHAPTER 23

Remaining Vigilant

The journey towards righteousness and spiritual maturity is not one of passivity, but of active, vigilant engagement. As believers, we are encouraged throughout scripture to *"be sober-minded; be watchful. Your adversary the devil prowls around like a roaring lion, seeking someone to devour"* (1 Peter 5:8). It becomes vital, therefore, for us to be both aware of the pitfalls that once ensnared us and equipped to avoid them in the future.

In the Old Testament, the Israelites were led by a pillar of cloud by day and a pillar of fire by night (Exodus 13:21-22). This was God's way of guiding His people, ensuring they didn't stray from the path He had set for them. Similarly, as New Testament believers, we are guided by the Holy Spirit. However, just as the Israelites had a responsibility to follow the pillars, we have a responsibility to remain attuned to the Spirit's guidance.

One of the most vital tools in our arsenal is the Word of God. David declares in Psalms 119:105, *"Your word is a lamp to my feet and a light to my path."* By immersing ourselves in scripture, we are fortifying our spirits, arming ourselves with the truth to counter the falsehoods the world, or our own flesh, might present to us. The term "lamp" in this scripture is translated from the Hebrew word "*ner*," which means a light, lamp, or candle. Just as a lamp illumines a dark path, God's Word provides clarity and direction in a world filled with confusion and chaos.

Equally crucial is regular and heartfelt prayer. Paul in 1 Thessalonians 5:17 succinctly commands us to *"pray without ceasing."* In Greek, the word for pray, *"proseuchomai,"* suggests an earnest turning towards God. Through prayer, we maintain our connection to God, allowing Him to alert us when we might be veering off course or warn us of potential pitfalls ahead.

Another significant aspect of vigilance is accountability. Just as Aaron and Hur held up Moses' hands during Israel's battle against the Amalekites (Exodus 17:12), we too need individuals who will support, correct, and guide us. These could be mentors, trusted friends, or spiritual leaders. Their perspective can often shine a light on blind spots in our lives that we might be unaware of.

The parable of the ten virgins in Matthew 25:1-13 underscores the importance of preparedness and vigilance. Five of the virgins were wise, taking oil with their lamps, while the other five were foolish, taking no oil. When the bridegroom was delayed, the foolish virgins ran out of oil and had to go buy some, missing the bridegroom's arrival. In ancient Greek, the term used for "wise" is *"phronimos,"* which means prudent or sensible. It implies an understanding and a mindful approach to situations. By actively preparing and staying vigilant, we can be like the wise virgins, ready for whatever comes our way.

We must also be wary of pride. After a period of growth and transformation, it can be easy to feel we have 'arrived' and let our guard down. Proverbs 16:18 warns, *"Pride goes before destruction, and a haughty spirit before a fall."* The Hebrew word for pride in this verse, *"ga'own,"* can mean exaltation or majesty but, in this context, indicates arrogance or pomp. Recognizing that we are always susceptible, that every day is a new opportunity for growth and also for potential pitfalls, keeps us humble and reliant on God's grace.

Recall the Apostle Paul's struggle, as described in Romans 7:15-20, where he laments about not doing the good he wants to do, but the evil he does not want to do. This internal battle, the dichotomy between the flesh and the spirit, underscores the need for continuous vigilance.

Lastly, fostering a heart of worship can act as a deterrent against ungodly trading. When our focus is on glorifying God, it becomes increasingly difficult to engage in actions that detract from that glory. The psalmist encapsulates this sentiment when he writes, *"Whom have I in heaven but you? And there is nothing on earth that I desire besides you"* (Psalm 73:25).

The road to maintaining vigilance is neither straightforward nor easy. It requires conscious effort, consistent engagement, and a heart turned towards God. But with these tools and principles at our disposal, we can navigate the journey, avoiding the snares that once held us captive.

In this journey of vigilance, community plays a pivotal role. The early church, as described in the Book of Acts, presents a beautiful portrait of believers living in harmony, sharing everything in common, and gathering regularly for worship and breaking bread (Acts 2:44-46). Such a close-knit community not only fosters deep relationships but also provides a network of safety against potential pitfalls. The phrase *"breaking bread"* from this scripture is translated from the Greek term *"klasma artou,"* emphasizing a sharing or a partaking together.

It's not just about a physical meal but a spiritual communion, a bond strengthened by a shared love for Christ.

As Hebrews 10:24-25 advises, *"And let us consider how to stir up one another to love and good works, not neglecting to meet together, as is the habit of some, but encouraging one another, and all the more as you see the Day drawing near."* The word "encouraging" in this passage comes from the Greek word *"parakaleo,"* which means to call alongside. It emphasizes the importance of drawing close to one another, urging fellow believers towards godliness and offering support in times of weakness.

Yet, community isn't just about drawing strength; it's also about providing strength. Galatians 6:1-2 speaks of restoring a brother caught in any transgression with a spirit of gentleness. The word "restore" is translated from the Greek term *"katartizo,"* which implies mending or refitting. Just as fishermen would mend their nets, believers are called to mend the spiritual breaches in their community. In doing so, we bear each other's burdens, fulfilling the law of Christ.

To further illustrate the importance of community and vigilance, consider the biblical account of Nehemiah and the rebuilding of Jerusalem's walls (Nehemiah 4). As the Israelites labored, they faced continuous threats from adversaries. Nehemiah's solution was a blend of faith and practicality. While the workers built with one hand, they held a weapon in the other. Half of the men stood guard, equipped for battle, while the others worked. In Hebrew, the term used for "stand guard" is *"amad mishmar,"* which suggests a vigilant, protective stance. This dual approach of work and watchfulness epitomizes the balance we must strike in our spiritual lives. We must be involved in the good work of the Kingdom while remaining vigilant against threats.

However, let's not forget the subtler threats that often go unnoticed. The gradual compromises, the small justifications, and the seemingly inconsequential choices we sometimes make can accumulate over time, leading us astray. Recall the cautionary tale of King Solomon. His love for foreign women led him to tolerate and eventually adopt their pagan practices, causing him to turn away from God (1 Kings 11:1-8). The Hebrew term for "turned away" in this passage is "*natah,*" implying a deliberate bending or inclining towards something. Solomon's decline was not abrupt but gradual, emphasizing the need for continuous vigilance in every aspect of our lives.

This brings us to introspection. Just as David prayed in Psalm 139:23-24, "*Search me, O God, and know my heart! Try me and know my thoughts! And see if there be any grievous way in me, and lead me in the way everlasting.*" This heartfelt plea reflects a deep desire for purity and a recognition of human frailty. The Hebrew term "*derak,*" translated as "way," can mean a path, journey, or manner of life. David is essentially asking God to scrutinize his life path and correct any deviations.

Incorporating such introspective prayers in our routine can aid in maintaining vigilance. Regular self-examinations, coupled with God's Word, act as spiritual diagnostics, highlighting areas that need attention.

Furthermore, remembering our past vulnerabilities and how God delivered us can serve as powerful reminders. In Numbers 15:37-41, the Israelites were instructed to make tassels on their garments' corners, serving as reminders to obey God's commandments and not follow after their own hearts and eyes, which had led them to immorality. While we may not wear physical tassels today, having symbolic or tangible reminders of our past failures and God's grace can keep us grounded.

The journey of vigilance is multifaceted, encompassing community, self-awareness, and active engagement with God's Word. It requires a conscious choice every day to walk in righteousness, rejecting the paths that once ensnared us. With the Holy Spirit as our guide, the Word as our light, and a community of believers by our side, we can traverse this path, growing ever closer to the image of Christ. The path may be narrow, and the gate may be small, but the reward is life everlasting.

CHAPTER 24

Embracing the Kingdom's Exchange

When Jesus began His earthly ministry, one of the primary messages He proclaimed was about the Kingdom of God. *"The time is fulfilled,"* He declared, *"and the kingdom of God is at hand; repent and believe in the gospel"* (Mark 1:15). This foundational proclamation offers profound insights into the theme of righteous trading. The term "kingdom" in Greek is *"basileia,"* which denotes royal power, kingship, dominion, or rule. When we speak of God's Kingdom, we're discussing His sovereign reign and rule in every aspect of creation, including the heart of man.

The heart of righteous trading is found in seeking and embracing this kingdom. For it is in this kingdom that the transactions are not based on worldly gains, but on eternal values. Jesus asked, *"For what will it profit a man if he gains the whole world and forfeits his soul?"* (Matthew 16:26). Here, Christ employs commercial language to pose a rhetorical question on the value of worldly gains compared to spiritual ones. He challenges our understanding of profit (Greek: *"kerdaino"*), asking us to weigh the ephemeral versus the eternal.

One can draw parallels to the rich young ruler (Matthew 19:16-22). He approached Jesus, asking about eternal life but left sorrowful upon hearing the cost. His attachment to wealth was a trade he wasn't willing to make. The word used for "sorrowful" in Greek is "*perilypos*," which denotes an encompassing sadness. His deep attachment to worldly possessions made the idea of an eternal kingdom's trade a difficult pill to swallow.

But what does it mean to trade in the kingdom's currency? It is to seek righteousness, peace, and joy in the Holy Spirit (Romans 14:17). The word "righteousness" in Greek is "*dikaiosyne*," indicating the state approved by God, which includes integrity, virtue, purity, and correctness in thinking and acting. This means that when we trade, we align our decisions, behaviors, and relationships with God's righteous standard.

However, this isn't a journey we embark on alone. Throughout Scripture, God has consistently provided guidance for those seeking to align with His will. Take the example of the Prophet Hosea. God instructed Hosea to marry Gomer, a woman prone to unfaithfulness, as a symbol of Israel's unfaithfulness to Him (Hosea 1-3). Hosea's obedient act of redeeming Gomer from the slave market becomes a powerful metaphor for God's redemptive love for Israel and humanity. In Hebrew, the word for "redeem" is "*ga'al*," which means to buy back by paying a price. This concept of redemption is a divine trade; God trades His mercy and grace for our sin and brokenness.

Moreover, the Lord's Prayer underscores this idea of Kingdom trading. When we pray, *"Your kingdom come, your will be done, on earth as it is in heaven"* (Matthew 6:10), we're expressing a desire for God's heavenly standards to manifest on earth. We're asking for an exchange: our human, flawed will for His perfect, righteous one.

The s tory o f M ary o f Bethany further i lluminates t his c oncept. B y pouring expensive perfume on Jesus' feet and wiping them with her hair, Mary made a profound trade (John 12:1-8). She exchanged a costly worldly possession for an act of deep devotion and worship. In contrast, Judas Iscariot criticized her, revealing his unrighteous trade of valuing money over genuine worship. The Greek word for the perfume's value, "*trimēnēs*," indicates something very precious. Mary's act symbolizes the value of trading temporal treasures for eternal intimacy with Christ.

In our pursuit of righteous trading, it's essential to realize that God's Kingdom operates on principles contrary to the world. Where the world emphasizes gaining, the Kingdom underscores giving. Where the world insists on revenge, the Kingdom advises forgiveness. The Beatitudes, as laid out in Matthew 5:1-12, beautifully encapsulate these Kingdom values. *"Blessed are the meek, for they shall inherit the earth,"* Jesus states. Here, "meek" in Greek is "*praus*," which doesn't mean weak but refers to exercising God's strength under His control. It's a gentleness, a restraint. Such principles, when embraced, lead to a life of righteousness and peace.

As we delve deeper into the Kingdom's values, we recognize that these aren't just abstract concepts but actionable truths that can transform our lives. Consider Zacchaeus, a chief tax collector, who, after encountering Jesus, declared, *"Behold, Lord, half of my goods I give to the poor. And if I have defrauded anyone of anything, I restore it fourfold"* (Luke 19:8). His declaration is not mere words but a commitment to righteous trading.

Embracing the Kingdom's exchange is a continuous journey, requiring us to assess and reassess our values, decisions, and actions in the light of God's Word. Through the Holy Spirit's guidance, the Word's wisdom, and the community of believers, we are empowered to embrace this righteous trade daily. The apostle Paul, a prime example of someone who underwent a significant paradigm shift in understanding value, once said, *"Indeed, I count everything as loss because of the surpassing worth of knowing Christ Jesus my Lord. For his sake I have suffered the loss of all things and count them as rubbish, in order that I may gain Christ"* (Philippians 3:8). Here, Paul uses the Greek word *"skubala"* for "rubbish," which indicates something considered worthless or detestable. What the world often treasures, when weighed against the splendor and intimacy of knowing Christ, becomes insignificant.

This recognition, however, is more than intellectual assent. It's a heart transformation. A realization that every earthly treasure pales in comparison to the richness of a life intertwined with the Creator. Such an epiphany often leads to profound moments of repentance and redirection.

If you're reading this and feeling the weight of past trades, trades that now seem futile and empty, know that it's never too late to embark on a journey towards righteous trading. God, in His infinite mercy and love, waits with outstretched arms, ready to guide, correct, and embrace. The prodigal son, upon realizing the emptiness of his pursuits, returned home, and was met not with scorn but with celebration (Luke 15:11-32). The father's joyous exclamation, *"For this my son was dead, and is alive again; he was lost, and is found,"* reveals God's heart towards those who choose to return.

Many of us, like the prodigal son, have ventured far, trading our inheritance for fleeting pleasures. Yet, the Father's heart remains the same. His love unwavering, His mercy unending. He doesn't see your mistakes; He sees a child, lost and wanting to come home.

If you're feeling this tug on your heart, an urge to redirect your life towards the Kingdom, towards righteous trading, do not suppress it. This very moment can be a defining one. If you haven't given your life to the Lord, if you haven't experienced the transformational power of His love, now is the opportune time.

A Prayer of Commitment

"Dear Heavenly Father,

I come before You, recognizing my past trades, acknowledging that many have been far from righteous. I've sought after the world, its pleasures, and its treasures, often sidelining the eternal for the temporal. But today, Lord, I desire a change. I want to trade rightly, to seek first Your Kingdom and righteousness.

Lord Jesus, I believe that You are the Son of God, that You died for my sins, and rose again, conquering death. I confess my sins, my wrong trades, and I ask for Your forgiveness. Cleanse me, renew me, and lead me on the path of righteousness.

I invite You into my heart, not as a mere guest, but as the Lord and King. Take control of my life, guide my decisions, and help me to align them with Your will. Fill me with Your Holy Spirit, that I might have the strength to resist the allure of worldly trades and embrace the values of Your Kingdom.

Thank you, God, for Your love, mercy, and grace. I commit to walking with You, learning from You, and trading rightly in Your Kingdom.

In Jesus' Name, Amen."

For all who prayed this prayer, know that heaven rejoices. A new journey begins today, one filled with hope, purpose, and divine trading. The

Kingdom's exchange is now at your fingertips, and as you walk hand in hand with the Savior, may every trade reflect the heart of the Father.

In this journey of life, moments will come when the world's allure might seem overpowering, but hold onto the promises of God, embrace the community of believers, and continuously immerse yourself in His Word. Therein lies the strength to trade rightly, to value the eternal over the ephemeral, and to truly embrace the Kingdom's exchange.

May the God of peace, who brought again from the dead our Lord Jesus, equip you with everything good that you may do His will, working in you that which is pleasing in His sight, through Jesus Christ, to whom be glory forever and ever. Amen. (Hebrews 13:20-21)